EXPLORERS

EYEWITNESS ACCOUNTS OF DARING
ADVENTURERS

BLUE MAGPIE BOOKS

**Blue
Magpie**

CONTENTS

INTRODUCTION

Ever since creatures that we would recognise as human walked out of Africa around 60,000 years ago, we have displayed an innate trait: an overwhelming desire to explore.

Those early homo sapiens ventured forth seeking new lands, food and opportunities (or perhaps just because they could), entering Eurasia first and then, over thousands of years, populating the far ends of the globe.

This passion for exploration and adventure has shaped and expanded our world ever since, with each epoch broadening the horizons of humankind. Prehistoric men and women ventured forth on foot from their caves wondering what was over the next hill. The invention of the wheel and the domestication of animals like cattle and horses extended man's reach on land. When the seas were mastered, mariners such as the Phoenicians and Carthaginians began exploring other continents and eventually mapped and circumnavigated our planet. When the skies were conquered, humans reached places more quickly and in greater numbers than ever before. When science made space travel possible, man went to the moon and dreamed of trips to distant planets. Who knows where our next steps will lead us?

While this wander lust has undoubtedly fuelled advances in human civilisation and created today's interconnected world, it has been a journey drenched with blood. Small wonder that the word travel originates from travail, to engage in painful or laborious effort, which in turn comes from the medieval Latin *trepalium,* an "instrument of torture".

So it is with many of the stories we have collected here. These are the eyewitness accounts of pioneering journeys undertaken by modern explorers, adventurers and conquerors, stretching across almost 600 years.

All involved considerable bravery, resourcefulness and indomitability. Many of them had an immense impact on the the world, helping to shape its future. Some also left death and destruction, slavery and exploitation in their wake, particularly for those whose land, people and treasures were often the objects of desire.

The only criteria we made for inclusion in this book was that the accounts had to be contemporaneous, written by people who were there at the time history was made. Such as the stories of the Spanish *conquistador* who helped slaughter the Aztecs in the mid-16th century, the physician who was at Columbus's side on his second voyage west in 1493, or the African-American Polar explorer who was one of two men to first reach the North Pole in 1909. These are their chronicles, in their own words, written at the time or shortly after their journeys occurred. While we have edited their accounts (often written in archaic language) to make them as understandable as possible to today's reader, we have sought to retain their meaning and authenticity.

The tales are often bloody, brutal and distressing, particularly those of the European colonialists setting out to "discover" lands and find alternative trade routes. Many were motivated not by some romantic ideals of being the first to reach new lands, to meet new peoples, to discover new information, but by greed; they and their backers - wealthy merchants and avaricious royals - wanted commercial gain, particularly gold and other treasures. When Francis Drake's *Golden Hind* returned in 1580 from plundering gold and silver from Spanish ships and garrisons in South America (who themselves had taken it from subjugated locals), the English galleon was so laden down with riches that she was in danger of sinking. Queen Elizabeth's half-share of the contraband was greater than the Crown's annual income; delighted, she threw a celebratory dinner aboard the Hind and knighted Drake. His other backers were said to have made a 4,700 per cent return on their investment in piracy.

Although often outnumbered, the Europeans possessed the advanced technology that enabled them to conquer and ransack as they saw fit: the spears, darts and rocks of the natives were no match for the armour, guns, crossbows and cannons of the invaders. The journeys of Columbus, Vespucci, Da Gama and others resulted in the wholesale slaughters of indigenous peoples in the Americas, Australia and elsewhere, and ushered in the slave trade and centuries of European colonial dominance, the scars of which remain with us today.

In justification, their enemies were dismissed as "savages" and "barbarians" who were little better than animals, though Spanish troops were astonished at the great cities built by the Aztecs, even as they attacked and destroyed them.

It is disturbing not only as judged through today's sensibilities: as the French philosopher Michel de Montaigne wrote in the mid-16th century: "Each man calls barbarism whatever is not his own practice." Europeans were blinding themselves to their own savagery; he argued that there was much more barbarity in someone being tortured to death limb-by-limb by religious fanatics during the Inquisition, than in someone being roasted and eaten after he was dead. His views, however, were not widely shared at the time.

Exploration is not always done for financial gain, of course, nor is it undertaken only by white Europeans, or only by men. Chinese and Arab explorers travelled widely across Asia and Africa (and probably the Americas) long before Europeans arrived, as our account of Vasco Da Gama's encounter with an Indian king illustrates. Perhaps the Islamic merchants who warned the king that the Europeans would "ruin his country" might be said to have had a point.

One of the greatest Arab explorers, perhaps the greatest traveller of pre-modern times and the father of the modern age of discovery, was the Moroccan-born 14th-century traveller Ibn Battuta, whose account here of his time living with the mercurial Sultan of Delhi in the mid-14th century is enlightening.

History, traditionally, has tended not only to be written by the victor, but also by the male of the species. During the centuries covered by this volume, women - European or not - were treated as second-class citizens, expected to stay at home, be dutiful wives, and raise children, while their menfolk went to war, discovered new lands and plundered them. There were, however, some admirable rebels to these strictures, and we include the accounts of four of them in this book, including from Isabella Bird, a 19th-century English explorer who became the first woman to be elected a Fellow of the Royal Geographical Society, and Ida Pfeiffer, an Austrian woman who, in the 1840s, decided to begin travelling the world at the age of 45. Less concerned with being first or planting flags, or killing, conquering and pillaging, their accounts bring a different and generally more insightful and thoughtful perspective to that of the men.

RICHARD BURTON - AMONG
MURDEROUS SOMALIS, 1854-55

∼

S ir Richard Francis Burton (1821–1890) was an English explorer, soldier, writer and diplomat who was particularly famous for travels in the Middle East and Africa, and his extraordinary knowledge of languages and cultures. According to one count, he spoke 40 European, Asian and African languages.

Burton's best-known achievements include a well-documented journey to Mecca in 1853, at a time when Europeans were forbidden access on pain of death, and an expedition with John Hanning Speke, when they became the first Europeans to visit the Great Lakes of Africa in search of the source of the Nile.

He was eccentric, egotistical, controversial and indefatigable, revelling in close personal contact with human cultures in all their variety and enjoying sexual adventures more suited to another age than that of prudish Victorian Britain. His works and letters also extensively criticised the colonial policies of the British Empire, often to the detriment of his career.

The son of a British Army colonel, Burton was an unruly

"gypsy-eyed" child, raised in France, Italy and England. Fiercely independent with an inherent disdain for authority and carrying an air of smouldering ferocity, he called himself "a waif, a stray... a blaze of light, without a focus", and complained that "England is the only country where I never feel at home". At 15, he was caught writing passionate letters to prostitutes. By his late teens, he was experimenting with opium, later saying that "opium taken in moderation is not a whit more injurious to a man than alcohol".

When, at age 21, he was expelled from Trinity College, Oxford, for breaking the rules, Burton decided he was "fit for nothing but to be shot at for six pence a day", and enlisted in the army, serving in India and, later, the Crimean war.

During a break in his military career, Burton persuaded the Royal Geographical Society to fund his attempting the Haj, a pilgrimage to Mecca and Medina. It was this journey, undertaken in 1853 disguised as an Afghan, that first made him famous.

The edited passage published here is the account he gave to the Royal Geographical Society of London about his expedition in 1854-55 to the fortress city of Harar (in present-day Ethiopia), which no European had before entered - indeed, there was a prophecy that the city would fall into ruin if a Christian were allowed in. Assuming at first the disguise of a Turkish merchant, Burton not only travelled to Harar but also was introduced to the Emir and stayed in the city for 10 days, officially as a guest but in reality as a prisoner. The journey back was plagued by a lack of supplies, and Burton wrote that he would have died of thirst had he not seen desert birds and realised that they would be near water.

While the expedition was camped near Berbera, his party was set upon by a group of Somali warriors. One fellow British officer was murdered, while Speke was captured and wounded in 11 places before managing to escape. Burton was impaled with a spear, the point entering one cheek and exiting the other, forcing him to flee with it still stuck in his head. He later described the Somalis as a "fierce and turbulent race".

Burton spent his later years working as a diplomat for Britain and continued to pursue exotic challenges. He searched for gorillas in the Congo (finding cannibals instead), and climbed mountains in Cameroon. In Brazil, he canoed down the São Francisco River, running rapids no man had previously survived.

He authored more than 40 books on his exploits, many of which became classics. His writings are unusually open and frank about his interest in sex and sexuality. He also translated the Kama Sutra *and* The Arabian Nights *into English - introducing stories such as* Aladdin *to the Western world.*

He died in Tunis of a heart attack in 1890 at the age of 69. He and his wife, Isabel, are buried in Mortlake, south-west London, in a tomb the shape of a Bedouin tent.

'THE HUMAN HEAD, ONCE STRUCK OFF, DOESN'T REGROW LIKE THE ROSE'

IN MARCH, 1854, after my return from Arabia to Bombay, I applied myself to the task of resuscitating the expedition. My plans were favourably received by Lord Elphinstone, the enlightened Governor of the Presidency, and by the local authorities, amongst whom the name of the Hon William Lumsden, then member of council, will ever be remembered with the liveliest feelings of gratitude and affection. In August, a despatch from the India House authorised the expedition. It was originally composed of three members - Lieut Heme of the 1st Bombay Europeans, Lieut Stroyan of the Indian Navy, and myself. The first-named officer was accustomed to survey, to daguerreotype, and to observe; and the second was distinguished by his surveys of the coast of Western India, in Sindh, and on the Panjab rivers. Soon afterwards, the expedition received an addition in Lieut J. H. Speke, of the 46th regiment Bengal N. I., who had spent many years in collecting the fauna of Tibet and the Himalayan mountains, and who volunteered with ardour to become a sharer in the hardships and the perils of African travel.

Assembled at Aden, in the summer of 1854, we found the public voice so loud against our project, that I offered as a preliminary to visit Harar in disguise, thus traversing the lands of the dreaded Eesa clan, and entering a place hitherto closed to us by a ruler with the worst of reputations. I could not suppress my curiosity about this mysterious city. It had been described to me as the headquarters of slavery in Eastern Africa, and its territory as a land flowing with milk and honey; the birthplace of the coffee-plant, and abounding in excellent cotton, tobacco, saffron, gums, and other valuable products. But when I spoke of visiting it, men stroked their beards, and in an Oriental phrase declared that the human head once struck off does not regrow like the rose.

Our arrangements were soon made. Lieutenant Speke was detached to Guray Bunder, with directions to explore, if possible, the celebrated Wadi Nogal, and to visit the Dulbahantas, most warlike of the Somal. Lieutenants Stroyan and Heme established their camp at Berbera, the great mart and harbour of the Eastern coast; and they employed themselves in ascertaining the productive resources of the country, in mastering the subject of slavery - still, I regret to say, flourishing in these regions - and in collecting carriage for a more extended journey. They were also directed, in case of my detention by the Emir of Harar, to demand restitution before allowing the great caravan, which supplies that city with the luxuries of life, to leave the coast.

In the meantime, I prepared for a trip into the interior. The political resident at Aden, our possession in the Red Sea, assisted me with two Somali policemen, and I provided myself with a small stock of cloth, tobacco, rice, dates, trinkets, and other articles with which a Moslem merchant would load his camels. I determined to travel as El Haj Abdullah, a personage of some sanctity. Perhaps my adventures and a short description of a city hitherto unvisited by Europeans may not be unacceptable to a Society which, though essentially scientific, does not withhold encouragement from the pioneer of discovery, reduced by hard necessity to use nature's instruments - his eyes and ears.

On the 29th October, 1854, I started from Aden in a Somali boat bound to Zayla, a small port on the African coast of the Red Sea, nearly opposite and about 140 miles from our Arabian settlement. After two days' sail we reached our destination, when I found that the mules, ordered three months before, and paid for, had not been procured. The governor, our old friend El Haj Shermarkay, sent immediately to the neighbouring port of Tajurrah; but between the delay of catching the animals and a contrary wind which delayed the vessel, I lost at Zayla twenty-eight days. Travellers, like poets, are mostly an angry race: by falling into a daily fit of passion, I proved to the governor and his son, who were profuse in their attentions, that I was in earnest.

HE SUPPLIED me with women (cooks), guides, servants, and camels - under protest, warning me that the road swarmed with brigands, that the Eesa had lately murdered his son,

that smallpox was depopulating Harar, and that the Emir or
prince was certain destruction. One death to a man is a
serious thing: a dozen neutralise one another. I contented
myself with determining the good Shermarkay to be the
true Oriental hyperbolist.

With four mules and five camels laden with cotton cloth,
Surat tobacco, rice, dates, various "notions", a few handsome
tobes or sheets (intended as presents to chiefs) and necessaries for the way, on the 27th November, 1854, El Haj Abdullah, attended by the governor, his son Mohammed, and a
detachment of Arab soldiers, passed through the southern
gate of Zayla, and took the way of the Desert.

There are two lines of road from Zayla to the ancient
capital of the Hadiyah empire. The more direct numbers
eight long stages through the Eesa territory, and two
through the mountains of the Nola tribe of Gallas. In this
country the "gedi" corresponds with the "hamlah" of Arabia:
it is a stage varying from four to five hours. The camels are
laden at dawn, and they proceed leisurely till about 10am,
when they are allowed to rest and feed. The march is
resumed in the afternoon, and at nightfall the beasts and
baggage are deposited in a thorn fence, which serves as a
protection against lions and plunderers. I estimate the
average progress to be 15 miles per diem; in places of danger
the Somal are capable of marching 27 or 28 miles without a
halt; on the contrary, when water and pasture abound, they
content themselves with a single short march. Shermarkay
objected to my travelling by the direct route on account of
the Eesa and the Gallas. These tribes inherit from their
ancestors the horrible practice of mutilation. They seek the
honour of murder, to use their own phrase, "as though it
were gain", and will spear a pregnant woman in hopes that
the unborn child may be a male. Then bearing with him his

trophy, the hero returns home and places it before his wife, who stands at the entrance of her hut uttering shrill cries of joy and tauntingly vaunting the prowess of her man. The latter sticks in his tufty poll an ostrich feather, the medal of these regions, and is ever afterwards looked upon with admiration by his fellows.

The route which I pursued is by no means direct; its sole merit is that, after a march of about 50 miles through the Eesa territory, the merchant enters the lands of the Gudabursi Somal, amongst whom life is, comparatively speaking, safe.

Our little caravan, consisting of about twenty well-armed men and two women cooks, was led by one *Ilaghe*, a petty chief of the Eesa tribe. Shermarkay had constituted him our *abban* or protector; in return for food and sundry presents of cloth and "notions", he afforded us a safeguard in the hour of danger. The "Abbanat", as it is called, is an intricate subject; I may describe it generally as a primitive and truly African way of levying custom-house dues. Your "protector" constitutes himself lord of your life and property; without him you can neither buy nor sell; he regulates your marches, and supplies you, for a consideration, with the necessaries of the road.

In six days, we traversed the maritime plain of Zayla; its breadth is from 45 to 48 miles. Along the shore all was desert, a saline flat warted with sand-heaps and bristling with a scanty salsolaceous vegetation. The sun singed as through a burning-glass, and the rare wells yielded a poor supply of bitter bilge-water. As we advanced inland, the country improved. Frequent fiumaras, or freshets, fringed with shrubs and thorn trees of the liveliest green, showed traces of the copious African monsoon. The ground was covered with a growth of yellow grass not unlike an English stubble; the kraals of the nomads appeared scattered over its surface; long lines of milch camels tossed their heads as they were being driven to pasture; numerous sheep, white as snow, flocked the plain; the beautiful little sand-antelope bounded over the bushes; and flights of vultures, unerring indicators of man's habitation in these lands, soared in the cloudless skies. Wherever we halted, we were surrounded by wandering troops of Bedouins. The coarser sex is almost black and exceedingly plain, but tall and well made: their frizzly hair is dyed dun by a mixture of ashes and water, and its only Macassar is a coat of melted sheep's fat. The toilette is simple - a dirty cotton cloth covering the loins, leather sandals, a round targe, a long dagger strapped round the waist, and two spears. The women are mostly habited in chocolate-coloured leather fringed at the border; their ornaments are zine earrings, armlets of the same material, a necklace of beads, and a fillet of blue cloth worn only by matrons. The girls plait their wiry locks into numerous little pigtails, and the heads of the naked children are shaved in a galeated fashion, with a crest of curly hair.

BY THE POWER of my star, I escaped a large plundering-party of Habr Awal horsemen, who were sweeping the plain with malicious intentions. A few rifle bullets would doubtless have beaten them off; in this land, if you clear two saddles per cent, the remainder will surely run. But pilgrims and peaceful travellers should avoid using carnal weapons, especially if they intend progress in Eastern Africa.

On the 3rd of December, we arrived at the southern frontier of the Eesa tribe, under the hills which form the first step to the highlands of Ethiopia and fringe the Somali coast from Tajurrah to Jerd Hafun or Guardafui; their formation is successively limestone, sandstone, and granite in the higher regions. The air became sensibly cooler, and we remarked an increased degree of fertility, together with traces of a monsoon which lasts from June to September in the torrent beds and cataracts which seam the faces of the hills. When I traversed this country it was a desert, the cold having driven the nomads to the maritime plain, but thorn fences and rings dotted the slopes, showing that in summer it is thickly inhabited. On the 7th December we threaded a fiumara, the primitive zigzag of these lands, and stood upon the summit of the maritime chain.

From the 7th to the 23rd of December, we traversed the country of the Gudabursi Somal, a large tribe, whose habitat is between the Eesa eastward and the Girhi to the W. Theirs is the rolling ground diversified with thorn-clad hill and fertile vale lying above the first zone of maritime mountain, and they have extended their lands by conquest towards Harar, being now bounded in that direction by the Marar Prairie. These nomads, who are said to number 10,000 shields, are rich in camels and cows; their warlike reputation depends upon a few wretched ponies. They are more hospitable and docile than the Eesa, but their brighter qualities are obscured by knavery, thievishness, exceeding covetousness, and a habit of lying, wonderful even to the Eastern traveller. Some of the girls are not wanting in attractions. I gave to one of the prettiest a bead necklace, and she repaid me by opining that I was painted white. The savages, who take a delight in sight showing, insisted upon my visiting the Halimalah tree and the ruins of Aububah and Darbinyah Kolah. The former is a gigantic fig (*Ficus religiosa*), under which is performed the ceremony of binding the turban around the brow of each newly-elected *Ugaz,* or chief. The ruins, composed of rough stones, the mud used for cement in these regions, and bars of wood inserted as in Kashmir between the courses of masonry, are interesting, as they prove that the land has not been always barbarous. The only tradition preserved by the nomads is, that the fort of Kolah - so called from its queen - as well as Aububah belonged to the Gallas, once lords of the soil, and that their violent hostility ended in mutual destruction.

In the Harawwah valley, I met with a notable disappointment as regards elephants. At Zayla they were represented to be plentiful as sheep; after beating the country nothing appeared but the last year's earths. The animals were still in the higher jungles, and we hastened to quit a place where it is impossible even to ride out without being covered with swarms of flies. The *tsetse* of Southern Africa does not exist here; there is, however, a red variety called *Diksi-As* (red fly), whose bite, according to the natives, is so hot in summer that it causes violent vomitings. This, together with the fever produced by the mosquito-sting, is universally believed by the people; the traveller will receive the information *cum grano*.

On the 23rd of December, I crossed the Ban Marar (Marar Prairie), a grassy tract not unlike our English downs, which separates the first from the second zone of hills. Its length is considerable; the breadth varies from 25 to 28 miles. The undulating surface is covered at this season with a glaring yellow coat of dried up grass; about half-way we halted for an hour in a wady or fiumara, where my Somal employed themselves in eating the acacia gum. The place is infamous for razzias, and a small caravan, laden with hides and clarified butter to be bartered for maize and grain, had the honour (as the phrase of the country is) to sit under the shade of our sandals. Starting at 6am, we arrived at 8 in the evening under the hills of Harar, with no other adventure than being dogged by a lion, who fled at the ring of a rifle. The cold was excessive, 42° in the hut at dawn, and in the noon sun the mercury rose to 120°.

THOUGH ALMOST IN sight of Harar, our advance was impeded by the African traveller's bane. The Gudabursi tribe was at enmity with the Girhi, and, in such cases, the custom is for your friends to detain you and for their enemies to bar your progress. Shermarkay had given me a letter to the Gerad Adan, chief of the Girhi; a family feud between him and his brother-in-law, our Gudabursi protector, rendered the latter chary of committing himself. We found ourselves forced to idleness until Dahabo, one of the chief's six wives, and his eldest son Sherwa, visited our kraal for the purpose of escorting us onwards.

On the 27th of December, we exchanged the rocks, thorn-trees, and dried grass of the desert for alpine scenery rendered by contrast truly delicious. We stood upon the portals of the highlands of Abyssinia, the huge primary chain which runs N. and S. along the length of Eastern Africa, and which - I hazard a conjecture - may have given rise to the theory of the "Lunatic Mountains".

This range is broken into abrupt masses, often with table-formed summits; mountain rills of the purest crystal bubble down the ravines, a system of fissures in the pink granite, and, collecting into one broad shallow stream, flow towards the Webbe Shebayli. A species of fir (the Sinaubar of India, here called Dayyib) clothes the flanks and summits of the hills which are bared of earth by heavy rains; its presence in these lands usually denotes an altitude of 5000 feet. The valleys were yellow with corn and tawny crops of the gigantic "Holcus Sorghum"; it was "harvest-home" when the song of the reapers and the sound of the flail gave pleasant proof that we had left the land of Bedouins. The roads were thronged with peasants and market-people, and in the hedges the daisy, the thistle, and the sweet briar were so many mementos of an English home.

We remained six days under the roof of the Gerad Adan, one of the most treacherous and dangerous chiefs in this land of treachery and danger. My Somali attendants saw with horror that preparations were being made to enter the city of evil fame. They attempted by all means in their power to deter me from the attempt, but the unfortunates little knew the persistency of a Haji. On the 2nd January, 1855, I mounted my mule, intending to enter Harar alone; the two policemen were shamed into accompanying me, and I left my third servant with the Gerad Adan, in charge of my heavy luggage and a letter of directions to be forwarded to Lieutenants Stroyan and Heme in case of accidents.

We passed on over the hills of Harar by roads so rugged that loads are shifted from camel to donkey back. As I approached the city, men turned out of their villages to ask if that was the Turk who was going to his death? The question made me resolve to appear before the Emir in my own character, an Englishman. In these lands it is a point of honour not to conceal tribe or nation, and, as a general rule, the Ottoman is more hated and feared than the Frank. On the 3rd of January, I entered Harar.

The ancient metropolis of the Hadiyah empire - now sadly decayed - is about 175 miles S.W. from Zayla and 219 S.W. from Berbera. My thermometer showed an altitude of about 5500 feet. The city lies upon the slope of a hill which falls from W. to E. In the latter direction are plantations of bananas, citrons, limes, the coffee-tree, the *kat* - a theine plant well known in Arabia - *wars*, or "bastard saffron", and sugar-cane. Westward are gardens and orchards on a terraced slope; northward is a hill covered with tombs, and to the S. the city falls into a valley or ravine. It is about one mile long by half that breadth; the streets and alleys are like mountain roads; and the abodes, built of sandstone and granite cemented with a reddish clay, present a dingy appearance, strikingly different from the glaring whitewash of the East.

The houses are flat-roofed, with small holes for windows and coarse wooden shutters; most of them have large courtyards and separate apartments for women, and almost all, even the Emir's palaces, are single-storeyed. There are some huts called "Gambisa", shaped like a bell-tent and peculiar to the cultivating Somal; they are equally common in Eastern and in Western Africa. The walls, ignorant of cannon, are defended by irregularly oval turrets whence spearmen and archers might annoy the enemy, and the five large gateways are full of guards armed with daggers and long staves. The climate appeared to me delightful - neither cold nor hot. Of eleven days we had three rainy; the air was fresh, and the sun not oppressive. The people assured me that their monsoon lasted six months, and this would account for the prodigious fertility of the soil.

The city owes its existence to the Emir Nur, who reigned about 316 years ago. In the days of Mohammed Gragne, the Attila of Eastern Africa, it was a mere collection of villages. The history of the place is a series of jihad or crusades against the pagan Gallas, and murder and sudden death of its petty princes. There are few public buildings: the bazar is a long street; the *jami* or cathedral mosque is a kind of barn decorated with two queer old minarets, built, it is said, by Turkish architects; and the palaces are single-storeyed houses with large courts, protected by doors of holcus stalks.

Harar contains a population of about 10,000 souls, including about 2500 Somal, and not including a considerable number of Gallas and other Bedouins. Women abound, a circumstance arising from the prevalence of slavery. Harar is the great "halfway-house" for the produce of Efat, Gurague, and the Galla countries; slaves are driven thence to Berbera and exported by the subjects of the Imam of Muscat, in exchange for rice and dates.

I did not judge favourably of the morals of the Harari. They drank freely - even in the presence of the Olema and pilgrims - hydromel and Farshu or Abyssinian beer. The Emir has been compelled to establish night patrols, who punish with the bastinado lovers and robbers. The men are peculiarly unprepossessing in appearance. Shaven heads, coarse features, and clumsy figures muffled in coarse *tobes* or sheets of dirty cotton cloth, with long thin staves in hand, frowned upon us with mischievous brows and occasionally addressed us with the roughest of voices.

The pretty Abyssinian features of the women were novel to me, and their utter ignorance of bashfulness a surprise. The dress is a long cotton robe, indigo-dyed, with two large inverted triangles of scarlet upon the chest and the shoulders: it is girt with a long zone of Harar manufacture. No veil is used, and sandals are at a discount. The hair, confined in blue muslin or network, is tied in two large bunches or balls below the ears, and the only ornaments are armlets of buffalo horn, coral necklaces, gilt hair pins, and Birmingham rings. Their voices are harsh, a phenomenon in Africa, where that organ is the only feature truly feminine; they chew tobacco with effrontery, drink beer, and demean themselves accordingly.

Harar is celebrated for sanctity, erudition, and fanaticism. The Shaykhs Abadil, El Bekri, and Ao Bahmah bequeathed to it a reputation. Of modern celebrities the Kabir Khalil and Kabir Yunis rank foremost. None but the purely religious sciences are studied, books are scarce, and there is no such thing as the *Wakf* or foundation for scholars, which makes men read in the East. Yet Harar sends forth a swarm of widad, *freres ignorantim*, who, by the power of long prayer and chanting the Koran, live, as such folk mostly aspire to do, in plenty and indolence.

Within the city, a language is spoken quite different from the Somali and the Galla dialects; like the former, however, it is partly Semitic in grammar and etymology, the Arabic scion being grafted upon an African stock. I collected a vocabulary and the grammatical forms which will afford the learned some idea of this still unknown tongue. The prevailing sound is the ch of the Scotch "loch," consequently the effect is harsh and unpleasant. Men of education always know Arabic, and the stranger hears in the streets Amharic, Galla, Somali, and Dankali.

The city is immediately surrounded by four tribes of Gallas, namely the Kola to the E. and N.E., the Alo on the W., the Babuli southwards, the Jarsa to the E. and S.E. It is impossible to see this people without remarking its consanguinity to the Somal. These Gallas are Christian, Moslem, and Pagan adoring *Wak* (the Creator), all living together without religious animosity. They might annihilate the city in a day, but it is not their interest to do so. The Emir pays them from 600 to 700 *tobes* per annum; they carry their lances into the palace-court, never run across His Highness's gateway, as all others must do, and drink gratis strong drinks which they have not the art to brew. In return they are plundered by the citizens, and the Emir has made it penal to buy by weight and scale.

THE GOVERNMENT MAY BRIEFLY BE DESCRIBED as the Emir. This petty prince, whose signet bears the grandiose title of "Sultan, son of Sultan", is by origin a Galla, by pretension a descendant from the Caliph Abubekr. He is a beardless youth, 23 or 24 years old, short, thin, and apparently consumptive; his wrinkled brow and protruding eyes give him an appearance truly unprepossessing. Men say that he was poisoned by one of his wives; others declare that his ill health is the effect of a fall from his horse.

He has four wives and two young children; during his three year reign he has imprisoned a selection from his fifty cousins, and as, in this city, political offenders are buried in a dark dungeon, confinement and death are nearly synonymous. The Emir preserves all the dignity of empire. Those presented to him must kiss the back and the palm of his hand. He must not be stared at - when his cough affects him, an attendant presents the hem of his robe. Rosaries are not allowed at the levee, and those presented are dragged by the arms to the foot of the throne. Running footmen precede the prince in the streets, flogging the people out of the way, and at mosque two or three matchlock men stand over him, for he fears internal treachery as much as external violence.

His *wazir*, the Gerad Mohammed, and his mother, the Gisti Fatimah, dare not address him without permission; he is, however, punctilious in administering justice. Imprisonment, fines, and the confiscation of property punish political offences. Murderers are given up to the nearest of kin, and their throats are publicly cut with a butcher's knife. Petty offenders are beaten in front and rear by two executioners armed with large horsewhips. Usually, the Emir allows his subjects to seek the benefits of the religious law as propounded by the Cazi Abd el Rahman. They prefer, however, the prince's prompt decisions. Generally in the East a man expects to be defrauded by the civil power, but he is morally certain of being stripped by the ministers of religion.

Harar is an essentially commercial town. Three caravans yearly convey to Berbera the rich spoils of the Galla country; those of January and February are small, that which leaves in the month of March consists of at least 3,000 souls and an equal number of camels. Ivory is a royal monopoly; the Emir buys it, and his subjects are forbidden to sell it. The best coffee comes from Jarjar, a Galla district about seven days W. of Harar. The *tobes* of this city are celebrated throughout Eastern Africa; handwoven, they far surpass the produce of our manufactures in beauty and durability. It is also the grand depot for the coffee, the wars-dye, the admirable cotton, the gums, the tobacco, and the grain of the Galla country. An idea of its cheapness may be formed from the fact that a dollar will purchase 120 fowls, and the same sum suffices to provide a man with bread for a year. The only coin is a bit of brass coarsely stamped; this "Mahallak" is the 66th part of a dollar, and the Emir imprisons all subjects who pass or possess any other money. Nothing can be more simple than the system of taxation; the cultivators pay 10 per cent, taken in kind, and traders are charged 16 cubits of cotton cloth per donkey load; the consequence is that the animal is supported through the gates by four or five porters.

After sitting for an hour at the eastern gate, waiting the permission of the Emir to enter his walls, we were ordered by a grim guard to follow. Arrived at the prince's courtyard, we were told to dismount and run, as the subjects of H. H. must never cross the gateway or approach the palace but at a long trot. I obeyed the former and resisted the latter order. Then, leading our mules, we stood under a tree close to the state prison, whence resounded the ominous clank of fetters, and turned deaf ears to the eager questions of the crowd. It was a levee-day, and troops of Galla chieftains, known by their heavy spears and zinc armlets, passed in and out of the palace prolonging our anxious delay.

At last, after being ordered to take off my slippers and to give up my weapons, a mandate to which I again objected, we were escorted by the grim guard to the palace-door. A curtain was raised. I entered with a loud *salam*, which was courteously returned by a small yellow man, not unlike an Indian Rajah, dressed in a conical turban and a red robe trimmed with white fur.

As I advanced towards the throne, four or five chamberlains seizing my arms, according to custom, hurried me on till I bent over the Emir Ahmed bin Abubekr's extended fingers. Leading me back, they then seated me in front of the presence, while my two Somali attendants were kissing the palm and the back of the thin yellow hand. Looking around the room, I remarked the significant decorations of its walls - bright fetters and rusty matchlocks. The courtiers stood in double file extended at right angles from the throne; all had their right arms and heads bared in token of respect, and whoever approached the Emir saluted his hand with exceeding reverence. At the end of my survey, I was called upon by the *wazir*, or prime minister, who sat upon a rug at the right of and below the throne, to answer a variety of questions concerning my name, nation, and business at Harar.

The replies proving, it is presumed, satisfactory, I was

invited to become the prince's guest during my ten days' residence, and received every day three dishes of bread and beef from his own kitchen. At subsequent visits, I was admitted to the honour of a seat next to the *wazir*, and the Emir did not disdain to be indoctrinated with the principles of free trade in coffee and cotton. Slavery was a more delicate topic, and not being authorized to treat upon the subject officially, I contented myself with observing its operations and with preparing a scheme which will easily and surely remove this curse upon the country's industry. During my residence at Harar, the two Somal who had been sent with me from Aden behaved admirably.

As smallpox was raging in the town, I found an easy pretext for hurrying my departure. These African cities are all prisons on a large scale. "You enter at your own bidding - you leave at another's" is the native proverb, true and significant. My speedy dismissal was perhaps owing to a report that three brothers had been sent by the Government of India to Eastern Africa. Visions of cutting off caravans induced the Emir to get rid of me, he being, it is said, much puzzled how to treat so uncommon a case. Yet I had no reason to complain of him; and as a proof that my modest endeavours to establish friendly relations were not unsuccessful, the Prince wrote, immediately after my departure to Aden, requesting to be furnished with a "Frank physician". He finally dismissed me with a mule for myself and a letter addressed to our Political Resident in Arabia.

I offer no description of my return route to Berbera, as it was a mere adventure of uncommon hardship. The accident which has for the present terminated our wanderings is deserving of some detail.

ON SATURDAY, the 7th of April, the H. E. I. Company's schooner *Main* (Lieut King commanding) entered the harbour of Berbera, where her guns roared forth a parting salute to the Somali expedition. The great emporium of Eastern Africa was, at the time of my second landing, in a state of confusion. But a few hours before the Harar caravan had entered; and purchase, barter, and exchange were being carried on in the utmost hurry. All day and during the greater part of the night the town rang with the loud voices of buyers and sellers. To specify no other valuable articles of traffic, 500 slaves of both sexes were in the market.

On the 9th of April, about 3pm, a shower, accompanied by thunder and lightning, came up from the southern hills, where rain had already been falling for some days, and gave notice that the Gugi or Somali monsoon had begun. This was the signal for the Bedouins to leave Berbera: the mats were rapidly stripped off their frameworks of stick and pole, the camels were laden, and thousands of travellers poured out of the town. On the 15th it was wholly deserted; the last craft left the port, and our little party remained in undisputed possession of the place. We awaited the mid-April mail. In their utter security, the *abbans* or protectors accompanied their families and property to the highlands, leaving with us their sons as an escort. The people were decidedly friendly: the most learned of the Somal, the Shaykh Jami, whom I had met at Harar, called repeatedly upon us, ate with us, and gave us abundant good advice concerning our future movements.

On the 18th April, a small craft belonging to the port of Aynterad entered the deserted creek, and brought from Aden ten Somalis, who desired to accompany us southwards. We objected to taking more than four of these men: fortunately, however, I ordered our people to give dinner to the captain and crew of the craft. That evening we were visited by spies, who deceived not only us, but even their own countrymen: accordingly, the usual two sentries were posted for the night, and we all lay down to sleep.

Between 2 and 3 in the morning of the 19th, I was aroused by the cry that the enemy was upon us. My first impulse was to request Lieut Heme to go out with his revolver in the direction of the attack; secondly, I called to Lieuts Stroyan and Speke that they must arm and be ready; and thirdly, I sent my servant for my sabre. Meanwhile, Lieut Heme returned hurriedly from the rear of the tent, exclaiming that our 12 servants, armed with swords and muskets, had run, and that the enemy amounted to about 150 men. Lieut Stroyan, who occupied another tent, did not appear: the other two officers and I were compelled to defend ourselves in our own with revolvers, which the darkness of the night rendered uncertain.

Presently our fire being exhausted, and the enemy pressing on with spear and javelin, the position became untenable; the tent was nearly battered down by clubs, and had we been entangled in its folds, we should have been killed without the power of resistance. I gave the word for a rush, and sallied out with my sabre, closely followed by Lieut Heme, with Lieut Speke in the rear. The former was allowed to pass through the enemy with no severer injury than a few hard blows with a war club. The latter was thrown down by a stone hurled at his chest and taken prisoner, a circumstance which we did not learn till afterwards.

On leaving the tent, I thought that I perceived the figure of the late Lieut Stroyan lying upon the ground close to the camels. I was surrounded at the time by about a dozen of the enemy, whose clubs rattled upon me without mercy, and the strokes of my sabre were rendered uncertain by the energetic pushes of an attendant who thus hoped to save me. The blade was raised to cut him down: he cried out in dismay, and at that moment a Somali stepped forward, threw his spear so as to pierce my face, and retired before he could be punished. I then fell back for assistance, and the enemy feared pursuing us into the darkness.

Many of our Somalis and servants were lurking about 100 yards from the fray, but nothing would persuade them to advance. The loss of blood causing me to feel faint, I was obliged to lie down, and, as dawn approached, the craft from Aynterad was seen apparently making sail out of the harbour.

WITH MY LITTLE REMAINING STRENGTH, I reached the spit at the head of the creek, was carried into the vessel, and persuaded the crew to arm themselves and repair to the scene of our disaster. Presently Lieut Heme appeared, and closely following him Lieut Speke, who had escaped from his captors, was supported in badly wounded. Lastly, the body of Lieut Stroyan was brought on board, speared through the heart, with the mark of a lance piercing the abdomen, and a frightful gash apparent in the forehead. The lamented officer had ceased to exist; his body was stark and cold. We preserved his remains till the morning of the 20th instant, when we were compelled to commit them to the deep, Lieut Heme reading the funeral service. We were overwhelmed with grief: we had lived together like brothers. Lieut Stroyan was a universal favourite, and truly melancholy was the contrast between the hour when he lay down to rest full of life and spirits, and the ensuing morning when we saw him a livid corpse.

In conclusion, I must remark that a number of little

combinations gave rise to our disaster. Our arrangements were hurriedly made. We could not take from Aden the number of well-trained

Somali policemen upon which I had originally calculated, and we had to depend upon raw recruits, who fled at the first charge. But we had ever been led to believe that Berbera was as safe as Bombay itself, and we expected, after a month's march, that the men would be educated to fight. Political events at Aden also prevented our detaining the war-schooner Mahi, whose presence would have rendered the coast safe, and once in the interior we should have been secure from the Bedouins, who have a horror of firearms. Had our letters despatched from Aden arrived when expected, we should have been enabled to leave Berbera with the Ogadayn caravan.

Yet my opinion of the Somal is unchanged; nor would I assume the act of a band of brigands - for such was the cause of our disaster - to be the expression of a people's animus. They have learned to respect us: four or five of their number were, it is reported, killed or mortally wounded that fatal night; and if my plans for punishing the outrage be carried out, it will be long before a similar event occurs again.

The officers whom I have had the honour to command profess themselves ready to renew the attempt; and when the ferment has subsided, we would start from Kurrum, a safer though a less interesting route. Should we be deterred by the loss of a single life, however valuable, from prosecuting plans now made public in Africa, we shall not rise in the estimation of the races around us. Briefly, permission to carry out our original projects is the sole recompense we hope for what we have suffered.

2

MATTHEW HENSON - JOURNEY TO THE NORTH POLE, 1909

*M*atthew Alexander Henson (1866-1955), an African American born on a Maryland farm to impoverished sharecroppers who had been free people of colour before the American Civil War, rose from being a dishwasher to become the co-discoverer of the North Pole and one of the 20th century's most admired explorers.

Henson had been a trusted companion of Robert Peary for more than 20 years when they set out on their eighth, and final, Arctic expedition, with 22 Inuit men, 17 Inuit women, 10 children, 246 dogs, 70 tons of whale meat, the meat and blubber from 50 walruses, hunting equipment, and tons of coal.

Peary, a US naval officer with a typically privileged white American background, had originally hired Henson as his personal valet, but grew to become dependent on his courage, intelligence, language abilities, and hard work. Peary - and many Inuits - admired Henson for his hunting and sledge-driving skills, as well as his ability to speak their language; the Inuits called him Mahri-Pahluk ("Matthew the Kind One"). Peary said, "He was more of an Eskimo than some of them."

In behaviour common to male Western explorers in those

years, Henson and Peary both took Inuit women as "country wives" and fathered children with them, as was common behavior. With a woman called Akatingwah, Matthew Henson fathered what was to be his only child, a son named Anauakaq. His children are Henson's only descendants. Similarly, Peary had a son, Kali, with his Inuit wife. Both boys were born in 1906.

Peary selected Henson as his final companion on the run-in to the Pole ahead of several white co-explorers. He said it had been an easy decision taken entirely on merit: "Henson must go all the way. I can't make it there without him." He later wrote that he had given Henson the position "primarily because of his adaptability and fitness for the work and secondly on account of his loyalty. He is a better dog driver and can handle a sledge better than any man living, except some of the best Esquimo hunters themselves."

The expedition had to endure temperatures of 65 degrees below zero, and cracking and drifting ice sheets that formed patches of open water called leads - "all the hells of this damned frozen land", as Henson put it.

Before the Pole was reached, Peary could no longer continue on foot and rode in a dog sled. Various accounts say he was ill, exhausted, or suffering from frostbite. He sent Henson on ahead as a scout.

Although he made no mention of this in his 1912 account of the expedition, A Negro at the North Pole, Henson later concluded that by dead reckoning he had reached the Pole 45 minutes before Peary arrived. He said he greeted his co-explorer with the words: "I think I'm the first man to sit on top of the world."

Henson recalled that this angered Peary. "Oh, he got hopping mad... No, he didn't say anything, but I could tell," he said. Peary simply "fastened the flag to a staff and planted it firmly on top of his igloo".

In a newspaper interview, Henson later recalled: "I was in the lead that had overshot the mark a couple of miles. We went back then and I could see that my footprints were the first at the spot."

In a sign of the times, however, all the glory of reaching the Pole went to Peary, despite questions that still endure today about whether the couple did reach the exact geographical spot. On their return to America, Peary was promoted to Rear Admiral, received many honors from scientific societies, served twice as president of the prestigious Explorers Club, and travelled the world as an acclaimed hero until his death in 1920, when he was buried at the Arlington National Cemetery.

In contrast, Henson spent the next three decades working as a humble clerk in a New York federal customs house. It was only at the age of 70, in 1937, that his long-overlooked achievements started to be recognised, when the Explorers Club made him an honorary member. In 1946, the US Navy awarded him a medal, identical to one given to Peary. In 1954, he was invited to the White House by President Dwight Eisenhower to receive a special commendation for his early work as an explorer.

He died, aged 88, in 1955, and was buried in a cemetery in New York. In 1988, by presidential order, his remains and those of his American wife, were re-interred with a monument at Arlington National Cemetery, near that for Peary and his wife. Among the guests were the descendants of both explorers' elderly Inuit sons, who had been tracked down two years earlier by an academic fascinated by Henson's story, and who brought them to America for a visit.

"We are assembled here today to right a tragic wrong, to right the record," S. Allen Counter, a Harvard professor of neurophysiology and a black history expert, stated at the event. "Welcome home, Matt Henson, to the company of your friend Robert Peary. Welcome home to a new day in America. Welcome home, brother."

The account published here is an edited extract of Henson's 1912 book, dealing with the final few days of the expedition.

∾

'WE WERE THE MEN WHO, IT HAD BEEN ORDAINED, WOULD UNLOCK THE MYSTERY OF THE ARCTIC'

MARCH 19: We left camp in a haze of bitter cold; the ice conditions about the same as the previous day; high rafters, huge and jagged; and we pickaxed the way continuously. By noontime, we found ourselves alongside of a lead covered by a film of young ice. We forced the dogs and they took it on the run, the ice undulating beneath them, the same as it does when little wanton boys play at tickley benders, often with serious results, on the newly formed ice ponds and brooks down in civilization. Our tickley benders were not done in the spirit of play, but on account of urgent necessity, and as it was I nearly suffered a serious loss of precious possessions.

One of the sledges, driven by Ahwatingwah, broke through the ice and its load, which consisted of my extra equipment, such as kamiks [sealskin boots], mittens, etc., was thoroughly soaked. Luckily for the boy, he was at the side of the sledge and escaped a ducking. Foolishly I rushed over, but, quickly realizing my danger, I slowed down, and with the utmost care he fished out the sledge, and the dogs, shaking as with palsy, were gently urged on. Walking wide, like the polar bear, we crept after, and without further incident reached the opposite side of the lead. My team had reached there before me and, with human intelligence, the dogs had dragged the sledge to a place of safety and were sitting on their haunches, with ears cocked forward, watching us in our precarious predicament. They seemed to rejoice at our deliverance, and as I went among them and untangled their traces I could not forbear giving each one an affectionate pat on the head.

For the next five hours, our trail lay over heavy pressure ridges, in some places sixty feet high. We had to make a trail over the mountains of ice and then come back for the sledges. A difficult climb began. Pushing from our very toes, straining every muscle, urging the dogs with voice and whip, we guided the sledges. On several occasions the dogs gave it up, standing still in their tracks, and we had to hold the sledges with the strength of our bones and muscles to prevent them from sliding backwards. When we had regained our equilibrium the dogs were again started, and in this way we gained the tops of the pressure-ridges.

Going down on the opposite side was more nerve-racking. On the descent of one ridge, in spite of the experienced care of Ootah, the sledge bounded away from him, and at a declivity of thirty feet was completely wrecked. The frightened dogs dashed wildly in every direction to escape the falling sledge, and as quickly as possible we slid down the steep incline, at the same time guiding the dogs attached to the two remaining sledges. We rushed over, my two boys and I, to the spot where the poor dogs stood trembling with fright. We released them from the tangle they were in, and, with kind words and pats of the hand on their heads, quieted them. For over an hour we struggled with the broken pieces of the wreck and finally lashed them together with strips of *oog-sook* (seal-hide).

We said nothing to the Commander when he caught up with us, but his quick eye took in at a glance the experience we had been through. The repairs having been completed, we again started. Before us stretched a heavy, old floe, giving us good going until we reached the lead, when the order was given to camp. We built our igloos, and boiled the tea and had what we called supper.

Commander Peary called me over to his igloo and gave me my orders: first; that I should at once select the best dogs of the three teams, as the ones disqualified by me would on the following morning be sent back to the ship, in care of the third supporting party, which was to turn back. Secondly; that I should rearrange the loads on the remainder of the sledges, there now being ten in number. It was 8pm when I began work and two the following morning when I had finished.

MARCH 20: During the night, the Commander had a long talk with [George] Borup, and in the morning my good friend, in command of the third supporting party, bade us all goodbye and took his detachment back to land and headquarters. There were three Eskimos and seventeen dogs in his party. A fine and plucky young man, whose cheerful manner and ready willingness had made him a prime favorite; and he had done his work like an old campaigner.

At the time of Borup's turning southward, Captain Bartlett, with two Eskimos, started out to the north to make trail. He was to act as pioneer. At 10.30am, I, with two Eskimos, followed; leaving at the igloos the Commander and Professor Marvin, with four Eskimos. The system of our marches from now on was that the first party, or pioneers, which consisted of Captain Bartlett, myself, and our Eskimos, should be trail-making, while the second party, consisting of Commander Peary and Marvin, with their Eskimos, should be sleeping; and while the first party was sleeping, the second should be traveling over the trail previously made. The sun was above the horizon the whole twenty-four hours of the day, and accordingly there was no darkness. Either the first or second party was always traveling, and progress was hourly made.

MARCH 21: Captain Bartlett got away early, leaving me in camp to await the arrival of Commander Peary and Marvin, with their party; and it was 8am when they arrived. Commander Peary instructed me to the effect that, when I overtook the Captain, I should tell him to make as much speed as possible.

The going was, for the first hour, over rough, raftered ice. Great care and caution had to be observed, but after that we reached a stretch of undulated, level ice, extending easily fifteen miles; and the exhilarating effect made our spirits rise. The snow-covering was soft, but with the help of our snow-shoes we paced off the miles, and at noon we caught up with the Captain and his boys. Together we traveled on, and at the end of an hour's going we halted for our noon-meal, consisting of a can of tea and three biscuits per man, the dogs doing the hungry looking on, as dogs have done and do and will do forever. As we sat and ate, we joshed each other, and the Eskimo boys joined in the good-natured raillery.

The meal did not detain us long, and soon we were pushing on again as quickly as possible over the level ice, fearing that if we delayed the condition of the ice would change, for changes come suddenly, and frequently without warning. At 9pm we camped, the Captain having been on the go for fifteen hours, and I for thirteen; and we estimated that we had a good fourteen miles to our credit.

MARCH 22 WAS the finest day we had, and it was a day of unusual clearness and calm; practically no wind and a cloudless sky. The fields of ice and snow sparkled and glistened and the daylight lasted for the full twenty-four hours. It was 6am when Egingwah, the Commander's Eskimo courier, reached our camp, with the note of command and encouragement; and immediately the Captain and I left camp.

Stretching to the northward was a brilliantly illuminated, level, and slightly drifted snow-plain, our imperial highway, presenting a spectacle grand and sublime; and we were truly grateful and inwardly prayed that this condition would last indefinitely. Without incident or accident, we marched on for fifteen hours, pacing off mile after mile in our steady northing, and at 9pm we halted. It was then we realized how utterly fatigued and exhausted we were. It took us over an hour and a half to build our igloos. We had a hard time finding suitable snow conditions for building them, and the weather was frightfully cold. The evening meal of pemmican-stew and tea was prepared, the dogs were fed, and we turned in.

MARCH 23: Our sleep-banked eyes were opened by the excitement caused by the arrival of Marvin and his division. He reported the same good going that we had had the day before, and also that he had taken an elevation of the sun and computed his latitude as 85°46' north. We turned the igloos over to Marvin and his Eskimos, who were to await the arrival of the Commander, and Captain Bartlett and myself got our parties under way.

Conditions are never similar, no two days are the same; and our going this day was nothing like the paradise of the day before. At a little distance from the igloos we encountered high masses of heavily-rubbled, old ice. The making of a trail through these masses of ice caused us to use our pick-axes continuously. It was backing and filling all of the time. First we would reconnoiter, then we would hew our way and make the trail, then we would go back and, getting in the traces, help the dogs pull the sledges, which were still heavily loaded. This operation was repeated practically all the day of March 23, except for the last hour of traveling, when we zigzagged to the eastward, where the ice appeared less formidable, consisting of small floes with rubble ice between and a heavy, old floe beyond. There we camped. The latitude was 85°46' north.

The course from the land to the Pole was not direct and due north, for we followed the lines of least resistance, and frequently found ourselves going due east or west, in order to detour around pressure ridges, floebergs, and leads.

MARCH 24: Commander Peary reached camp shortly after 6am, and after a few brief instructions, we started out. The going not as heavy as the day previous; but the sky overcast, and a heavy drift on the surface made it decidedly unpleasant for the dogs. For the first six hours the going was over rough, jagged ice, covered with deep, soft snow; for the rest of the day it improved. We encountered comparatively level ice, with a few hummocks, and in places covered with deep snow. We camped at 8pm, beside a very heavy pressure-ridge as long as a city street and as high as the houses along the street.

MARCH 25: Turned out at 4.30am, to find a steadily falling snow storm upon us. We breakfasted, and fifteen minutes later we were once more at work making trail. Our burly neighbor, the pressure-ridge, in whose lee we had spent the night, did not make an insuperable obstacle, and in the course of an hour we had made a trail across it, and returned to the igloo for the sledges. We found that the main column had reached camp, and after greetings had been given, Commander Peary called me aside and gave me my orders; to take the trail at once, to speed it up to the best of my ability and cover as much distance as possible; for he intended that I should remain at the igloo the following day to sort out the best dogs and rearrange the loads, as Marvin was to turn back with the fourth supporting party. My heart stopped palpitating, I breathed easier, and my mind was relieved. It was not my turn yet, I was to continue onward and there only remained one person between me and the Pole - the Captain. We knew Commander Peary's general plan: that, at the end of certain periods, certain parties would turn south to the land and the ship; but we did not know who would comprise or command those parties and, until I had the Commander's word, I feared that I would be the next after Borup. At the same time, I did not see how Marvin could travel much longer, as his feet were very badly frozen.

Obedient to the Commander's orders, the Captain, I, and our Eskimos, left camp with loaded sledges and trudged over the newly made trail, coming to rough ice which stretched for a distance of five miles, and kept us hard at back-straining, shoulder-wrenching work for several hours. The rest of the day's march was over level, unbroken, young ice; and the distance covered was considerable.

MARCH 26: The Commander and party reached the igloo at 10.45am. Captain Bartlett had taken to the trail at six and was now miles to the northward, out of sight. I immediately started to work on the task assigned me by the Commander, assorting the dogs first, so that the different king dogs could fight it out and adjust themselves to new conditions while I was rearranging the loads.

At twelve noon, Professor Marvin took his final sight, and after figuring it out told me that he made it 86°38' north. The work of readjusting the loads kept me busy until 7pm. While doing this work I came across my Bible that I had neglected so long, and that night, before going to sleep, I read the twenty-third Psalm, and the fifth chapter of St Matthew.

MARCH 27: I was to take the trail at 6am, but before starting I went over to Marvin's igloo to bid him goodbye. In his quiet, earnest manner, he advised me to keep on, and hoped for our success; he congratulated me and we gave each other the strong, fraternal grip of our honored fraternity and we confidently expected to see each other again at the ship. My good, kind friend was never again to see us, or talk with us. It is sad to write this. He went back to his death, drowned in the cold, black water of the Big Lead. In unmarked, unmarbled grave, he sleeps his last, long sleep.

Leaving the Commander and Marvin at the igloos, my party took up the Captain's trail northward. It was expected that Peary would follow in an hour and that at the same time Marvin would start his return march. After a few minutes' going, we came to young ice of this season, broken up and frozen solid, not difficult to negotiate, but requiring constant pulling; leaving this, we came to an open lead which caused us to make a detour to the westward for four miles. We crossed on ice so thin that one of the sledge-runners broke through, and a little beyond one of the dogs fell in so completely that it was a precarious effort to rescue him; but we made it and, doglike, he shook the water out of his fur and a little later, when his fur froze, I gave him a thorough beating; not for falling in the water, but in order to loosen the ice particles, so that he could shake them off. Poor brute, it was no use, and in a short while he commenced to develop symptoms of the dread *piblokto* [a kind of hysterical reaction], so in mercy he was killed. One of the Eskimo boys did the killing.

Dangerous as the crossing was, it was the only place possible, and we succeeded far better than we had anticipated. Beyond the lead we came to an old floe and, beyond that, young ice of one season's formation, similar to that which had been encountered earlier in the day. Before us lay a heavy, old floe, covered with soft, deep snow in which we sank continually; but it was only 5pm when we reached the Captain's igloo. Anticipating the arrival of the Commander, we built another igloo, and about an hour and a half later the Commander and his party came in.

MARCH 28: Exactly 40° below zero when we pushed the sledges up to the curled-up dogs and started them off over rough ice covered with deep soft snow. It was like walking in loose granulated sugar. Indeed I might compare the snow of the Arctic to the granules of sugar, without their saccharine sweetness, but with freezing cold instead; you can not make snowballs of it, for it is too thoroughly congealed, and when it is packed by the wind it is almost as solid as ice. It is from the packed snow that the blocks used to form the igloo-walls are cut.

At the end of four hours, we came to the igloo where the Captain and his boys were sleeping the sleep of utter exhaustion. In order not to interrupt the Captain's rest, we built another igloo and unloaded his sledge, and distributed the greater part of the load among the sledges of the party. The Captain, on awakening, told us that the journey we had completed on that day had been made by him under the most trying conditions, and that it had taken him fourteen hours to do it. We were able to make better time because we had his trail to follow, and, therefore, the necessity of finding the easiest way was avoided. That was the object of the scout or pioneer party and Captain Bartlett had done practically all of it up to the time he turned back at 87°48' north.

MARCH 29: You have undoubtedly taken into consideration the pangs of hunger and of cold that you know assailed us, going Pole-ward; but have you ever considered that we were thirsty for water to drink or hungry for fat? To eat snow to quench our thirst would have been the height of folly, and as well as being thirsty, we were continuously assailed by the pangs of a hunger that called for the fat, good, rich, oily, juicy fat that our systems craved and demanded.

Had we succumbed to the temptations of thirst and eaten the snow, we would not be able to tell the tale of the conquest of the Pole; for the result of eating snow is death. True, the dogs licked up enough moisture to quench their thirst, but we were not made of such stern stuff as they. Snow would have reduced our temperatures and we would quickly have fallen by the way. We had to wait until camp was made and the fire of alcohol started before we had a chance, and it was with hot tea that we quenched our thirst. The hunger for fat was not appeased; a dog or two was killed, but his carcass went to the Eskimos and the entrails were fed to the rest of the pack. We ate no dogs on this trip, for various reasons, mainly, that the eating of dog is only a last resort, and we had plenty of food, and raw dog is flavorless and very tough. The killing of a dog is such a horrible matter that I will not describe it, and it is permitted only when all other exigencies have been exhausted. An Eskimo does not permit one drop of blood to escape.

The morning of the 29th of March, 1909, a heavy and dense fog of frost spicules overhung the camp. At 4am, the Captain left camp to make as far a northing as possible. I with my Eskimos followed later. On our way we passed over very rough ice alternating with small floes, young ice of a few months duration, and one old floe. We were now beside a lead of over three hundred feet in width, which we were unable to cross at that time because the ice was running steadily, though to the Northward. Following the trail of the Captain, which carried us a little to the westward of the lead, within one hundred feet of the Captain's igloo, the order to camp was given, as going forward was impossible. The whole party was together farther north than had ever been made by any other human beings, and in perfectly good condition; but the time was quickly coming when the little party would have to be made smaller and some part of it sent back. We were too fatigued to argue the question.

We turned in for a rest and sleep, but soon turned out again in pandemonium incomprehensible; the ice moving in all directions, our igloos wrecked, and every instant our very lives in danger. With eyes dazed by sleep, we tried to guide the terror-stricken dogs and push the sledges to safety, but rapidly we saw the party being separated and the black water begin to appear amid the roar of the breaking ice floes.

To the westward of our igloo stood the Captain's igloo, on an island of ice, which revolved, while swiftly drifting to the east. On one occasion the floe happened to strike the main floe. The Captain, intently watching his opportunity, quickly crossed with his Eskimos. He had scarcely set foot on the opposite floe when the floe on which he had been previously isolated swung off, and rapidly disappeared.

Once more the parties were together. Thoroughly exhausted, we turned in and fell asleep, myself and the Eskimos too dumb for utterance, and Commander Peary and Bartlett too full of the realization of our escape to have much to say. The dogs were in very good condition, taking everything into consideration.

When we woke up it was the morning of another day, March 30, and we found open water all about us. We could not go on until either the lead had frozen or until it had raftered shut. Temperature 35° below zero, and the weather clear and calm with no visible motion of the ice. We spent the day industriously in camp, mending foot-gear, harness, clothing, and looking after the dogs and their traces. This was work enough, especially untangling the traces of the bewildered dogs. The traces, snarled and entangled, besides being frozen to the consistency of wire, gave us the hardest work; and owing to the activity of the dogs in leaping and bounding over each other, we had the most unideal conditions possible to contend with, and we were handicapped by having to use mitted instead of ungloved fingers to untangle the snarls of knots. Unlike Alexander the Great, we dared not cut the "Gordian Knots", but we did get them untangled.

About five o'clock in the afternoon, the temperature had

fallen to 43° below zero, and at the same time the ice began to move again. Owing to the attraction of the moon, the mighty flanks of the earth were being drawn by her invisible force, and were commencing again to crack and be rent asunder.

We loaded up hurriedly and all three parties left the camp and crossed over the place where recently had been the open lead, and beyond for more than five miles, until we reached the heavier and solid ice of the large floes. Northward our way led, and we kept on in that direction accordingly, at times crossing young ice so thin that the motion of the sledges would cause the ice to undulate. Over old floes of the blue, hummocky kind, on which the snow had fallen and become packed solid, the rest of this day's journey was completed. We staggered into camp like drunken men, and built our igloos by force of habit rather than with the intelligence of human beings.

It was continuously daylight, but such a light as never was on land or sea. The next day was April 1, and the Farthest North of Bartlett. I knew at this time that he was to go back, and that I was to continue, so I had no misgivings and neither had he. He was ready and anxious to take the back trail. His five marches were up and he was glad of it, and he was told that in the morning he must turn back and knit the trail together, so that the main column could return over a beaten path.

Before going to sleep, Peary and he (Captain Bartlett) had figured out the reckoning of the distance, and, to insure the Captain's making at least 88° north, Peary let him have another go, for a short distance northward, and at noon on the day of his return, the observations showed that Captain Bartlett had made 87°47' North Latitude, or practically 88° north. "Why, Peary," he said, "it is just like every day", and so it was, with this exception, like every day in the Arctic, but with all of every day's chances and hazards. The lion-like month of March had passed. Captain Bartlett bade us all farewell. He turned back from the Farthest North that had ever been reached by any one, to insure the safe return of him who was to go to a still Farther North, the very top of the world, the Pole itself.

While waiting for Bartlett to return from his forced march, the main party had been at work, assorting dogs (by this time without much trouble, as only one was found utterly unfit to make progress), and rearranging loads, for the Captain had almost three hundred miles of sea-ice to negotiate before he would reach terra firma, and he had to have his food-supply arranged so that it would carry him to the land and back to the ship, and dogs in good enough condition to pull the loads, as well as enough sledges to bear his equipment. When he did come back to our camp, before the parting, he was perfectly satisfied, and with the same old confidence he swept his little party together and at 3pm, with a cheery "Goodbye! Good Luck!" he was off. His Eskimo boys, attempting in English, too, gave us their "Goodbyes". The least emotional of all of our partings; and this brave man, who had borne the brunt of all of the hardships, like the true-blue, dead-game, unconquerable hero that he was, set out to do the work that was left for him to do; to knit the broken strands of our upward trail together, so that we who were at his rear could follow in safety. I have never heard the story of the return of Captain Bartlett in detail; his Eskimo boys were incapable of telling it, and Captain Bartlett is altogether too modest.

Captain Bartlett and his two boys had commenced their return journey, and the main column, depleted to its final strength, started northward. We were six: Peary, the commander, the Eskimos, Ootah, Egingwah, Seegloo and Ooqueah, and myself.

Day and night were the same. My thoughts were on the going and getting forward, and on nothing else. The wind was from the southeast, and seemed to push us on, and the sun was at our backs, a ball of livid fire, rolling his way above the horizon in never-ending day.

The Captain had gone. Commander Peary and I were alone (save for the four Eskimos), the same as we had been so often in the past years, and as we looked at each other we realized our position and we knew without speaking that the time had come for us to demonstrate that we were the men who, it had been ordained, should unlock the door which held the mystery of the Arctic. Without an instant's hesitation, the order to push on was given, and we started off in the trail made by the Captain to cover the Farthest North he had made and to push on over one hundred and thirty miles to our final destination.

The Captain had had rough going, but, owing to the fact that his trail was our track for a short time, and that we came to good going shortly after leaving his turning point, we made excellent distance without any trouble, and only stopped when we came to a lead barely frozen over, a full twenty-five miles beyond. We camped and waited for the strong southeast wind to force the sides of the lead together. The Eskimos had eaten a meal of stewed dog, cooked over a fire of wood from a discarded sledge, and, owing to their wonderful powers of recuperation, were in good condition; Commander Peary and myself, rested and invigorated by our thirty hours in the last camp, waiting for the return and departure of Captain Bartlett, were also in fine fettle, and accordingly the accomplishment of twenty-five miles of northward progress was not exceptional. With my proven ability in gauging distances, Commander Peary was ready to take the reckoning as I made it and he did not resort to solar observations until we were within a hand's grasp of the Pole.

The memory of those last five marches, from the Farthest North of Captain Bartlett to the arrival of our party at the Pole, is a memory of toil, fatigue, and exhaustion, but we were urged on and encouraged by our relentless commander, who was himself being scourged by the final lashings of the dominating influence that had controlled his life. From the land to 87°48' north, Commander Peary had had the best of the going, for he had brought up the rear and had utilized the trail made by the preceding parties, and thus he had kept himself in the best of condition for the time when he made the spurt that brought him to the end of the race. From 87°48' north, he kept in the lead and did his work in such a way as to convince me that he was still as good a man as he had ever been. We marched and marched, falling down in our tracks repeatedly, until it was impossible to go on. We were forced to camp, in spite of the impatience of the Commander, who found himself unable to rest, and who only waited long enough for us to relax into sound sleep, when he would wake us up and start us off again. I do not believe that he slept for one hour from April 2 until after he had loaded us up and ordered us to go back over our old trail, and I often think that from the instant when the order to return was given until the land was again sighted, he was in a continual daze.

Onward we forced our weary way. Commander Peary took his sights from the time our chronometer-watches gave, and I, knowing that we had kept on going in practically a straight line, was sure that we had more than covered the necessary distance to insure our arrival at the top of the earth.

It was during the march of the 3rd of April that I endured an instant of hideous horror. We were crossing a lane of moving ice. Commander Peary was in the lead setting the pace, and a half hour later the four boys and myself followed in single file. They had all gone before, and I was standing and pushing at the upstanders of my sledge, when the block of ice I was using as a support slipped from underneath my feet, and before I knew it the sledge was out of my grasp, and I was floundering in the water of the lead. I did the best I could. I tore my hood from off my head and struggled frantically. My hands were gloved and I could not take hold of the ice, but before I could give the "Grand Hailing Sign of Distress", faithful old Ootah had grabbed me by the nape of the neck, the same as he would have grabbed a dog, and with one hand he pulled me out of the water, and with the other hurried the team across.

He had saved my life, but I did not tell him so, for such occurrences are taken as part of the day's work, and the sledge he safeguarded was of much more importance, for it held, as part of its load, the Commander's sextant, the mercury, and the coils of piano-wire that were the essential portion of the scientific part of the expedition. My *kamiks* (sealskin boots) were stripped off, and the congealed water was beaten out of my bearskin trousers, and with a dry pair of *kamiks*, we hurried on to overtake the column. When we caught up, we found the boys gathered around the Commander, doing their best to relieve him of his discomfort, for he had fallen into the water also, and while he was not complaining, I was sure that his bath had not been any more voluntary than mine had been.

WHEN WE HALTED on April 6, 1909, and started to build the

igloos, the dogs and sledges having been secured, I noticed Commander Peary at work unloading his sledge and unpacking several bundles of equipment. He pulled out from under his *kooletah* (thick, fur outer-garment) a small folded package and unfolded it. I recognized his old silk flag, and realized that this was to be a camp of importance. Our different camps had been known as Camp Number One, Number Two, etc., but after the turning back of Captain Bartlett, the camps had been given names such as Camp Nansen, Camp Cagni, etc., and I asked what the name of this camp was to be - "Camp Peary?" "This, my boy, is to be Camp Morris K. Jesup, the last and most northerly camp on the earth." He fastened the flag to a staff and planted it firmly on the top of his igloo. For a few minutes it hung limp and lifeless in the dead calm of the haze, and then a slight breeze increasing in strength, caused the folds to straighten out, and soon it was rippling out in sparkling color. The stars and stripes were "nailed to the Pole".

A thrill of patriotism ran through me and I raised my voice to cheer the starry emblem of my native land. The Eskimos gathered around and, taking the time from Commander Peary, three hearty cheers rang out on the still, frosty air, our dumb dogs looking on in puzzled surprise. As prospects for getting a sight of the sun were not good, we turned in and slept, leaving the flag proudly floating above us.

This was a thin silk flag that Commander Peary had carried on all of his Arctic journeys, and he had always flown it at his last camps. It was as glorious and as inspiring a banner as any battle-scarred, blood-stained standard of the world — and this badge of honor and courage was also blood-stained and battle-scarred, for at several places there were blank squares marking the spots where pieces had been cut out at each of the "Farthests" of its brave bearer, and left with the records in the cairns, as mute but eloquent witnesses of his achievements. At the North Pole a diagonal strip running from the upper left to the lower right corner was cut and this precious strip, together with a brief record, was placed in an empty tin, sealed up and buried in the ice, as a record for all time.

Commander Peary also had another American flag, sewn on a white ground, and it was the emblem of the "Daughters of the Revolution Peace Society"; he also had and flew the emblem of the Navy League, and the emblems of a couple of college fraternities of which he was a member.

It was about 10 or 10.30am, on the 7th of April, 1909, that the Commander gave the order to build a snow-shield to protect him from the flying drift of the surface-snow. I knew that he was about to take an observation, and while we worked I was nervously apprehensive, for I felt that the end of our journey had come. When we handed him the pan of mercury, the hour was within a very few minutes of noon. Laying flat on his stomach, he took the elevation and made the notes on a piece of tissue-paper at his head. With sun-blinded eyes, he snapped shut the vernier (a graduated scale that subdivides the smallest divisions on the sector of the circular scale of the sextant) and with the resolute squaring of his jaws, I was sure that he was satisfied, and I was confident that the journey had ended. Feeling that the time had come, I ungloved my right hand and went forward to congratulate him on the success of our eighteen years of effort, but a gust of wind blew something into his eye, or else the burning pain caused by his prolonged look at the reflection of the limb of the sun forced him to turn aside; and with both hands covering his eyes, he gave us orders to not let him sleep for more than four hours, for six hours later he purposed to take another sight about four miles beyond, and that he wanted at least two hours to make the trip and get everything in readiness.

I unloaded a sledge, and reloaded it with a couple of skins, the instruments, and a cooker with enough alcohol and food for one meal for three, and then I turned into the igloo where my boys were already sound asleep. The thermometer registered 29° below zero. I fell into a dreamless sleep and slept for about a minute, so I thought, when I was awakened by the clatter and noise made by the return of Peary and his boys.

The Commander gave the word, "We will plant the stars and stripes at the North Pole" and it was done; on the peak of a huge paleocrystic floeberg, the glorious banner was unfurled to the breeze, and as it snapped and crackled with the wind, I felt a savage joy and exultation. Another world's accomplishment was done and finished, and as in the past, from the beginning of history, wherever the world's work was done by a white man, he had been accompanied by a coloured man. From the building of the pyramids and the journey to the Cross, to the discovery of the new world and the discovery of the North Pole, the Negro had been the faithful and constant companion of the Caucasian, and I felt all that it was possible for me to feel, that it was I, a lowly member of my race, who had been chosen by fate to represent it, at this, almost the last of the world's great work.

The four Eskimos who stood with Commander Peary at the North Pole, were the brothers, Ootah and Egingwah, the old campaigner, Seegloo, and the sturdy, boyish Ooqueah. Four devoted companions, blindly confident in the leader, they worked only that he might succeed and for the promise of reward that had been made before they had left the ship, which promise they were sure would be kept. Together with the faithful dogs, these men had insured the success of the master. They had all of the characteristics of the dogs, including the dogs' fidelity. Within their breasts lingered the same infatuations that Commander Peary seemed to inspire in all who were with him, and though frequently complaining and constantly requiring to be urged to do their utmost, they worked faithfully and willingly. Ootah, of my party, was the oldest, a married man, of about thirty-four years, and regarded as the best all around member of the tribe, a great hunter, a kind father, and a good provider. Owing to his strong character and the fact that he was more easily managed by me than by any of the others, he had been a member of my party from the time we left the ship. Without exaggeration, I can say that we had both saved each other's lives more than once, but it had all gone in as part of the day's work, and neither of us dwelt on our obligations to the other.

My other boy, Ooqueah, was a young man of about nineteen or twenty, very sturdy and stocky of build, and with an open, honest countenance, a smile that was "childlike and bland", and a character that was childlike and bland. It was alleged that the efforts of young Ooqueah were spurred on by the shafts of love, and that it was in the hopes of winning the hand of the demure Miss Anadore, the charming daughter of Ikwah, the first Eskimo of Commander Peary's acquaintance, that he worked so valiantly. His efforts were of an ardent character, but it was not due to the ardor of love, as far as I could see, but to his desire to please and his anxiety to win the promised rewards that would raise him to the grade of a millionaire, according to Eskimo standards.

Commander Peary's boy, Egingwah, was the brother of my boy Ootah, also married and of good report in his community, and it was he who drove the Morris K. Jesup sledge. If there was any sentiment among the Eskimos in regard to the success of the venture, Ootah and Seegloo by their unswerving loyalty and fidelity expressed it. They had been members of the "Farthest North party" in 1906, the party that was almost lost beyond and in the "Big Lead", and only reached the land again in a state of almost complete collapse. They were the ones who, on bidding Commander Peary farewell in 1906, when he was returning a saddened and discouraged man, told him to be of good cheer and that when he came back again, Ootah and Seegloo would go along, and stay until Commander Peary had succeeded, and they did. The cowardice of their fellow Eskimos at the "Big Lead" on this journey did not in the least demoralize them, and when they were absolutely alone on the trail, with every chance to turn back and return to comfort, wife, and family, they remained steadfast and true, and ever northward guided their sledges.

3

ISABELLA BIRD -THE ASSASSINATION
OF THE KOREAN QUEEN, 1895

*I*sabella Lucy Bird (1831-1904), was a 19th-century English explorer, who, in 1892, became the first woman to be elected a Fellow of the Royal Geographical Society. At a time when most women were expected to stay at home and raise children, Bird was an intrepid explorer and her chronicles of the countries she visited and the people she met made her a household name. Her story is even more remarkable in that she was a sickly child, suffering from a spinal complaint, nervous headaches, and insomnia.

In 1854, her father gave her £100 and told her that she was free to go wherever she wanted. She used it to travel to America to visit relatives, and her first book, An Englishwoman in America, was published in 1856. She later went back to the US to live in the Rocky Mountains, where she became friendly with Jim Nugent, "Rocky Mountain Jim", a one-eyed outlaw with a penchant for violence and poetry. Nugent, captivated by Bird, asked her to marry him, but she reluctantly declined, later writing that he was "a man any woman might love but no sane woman would marry". Nugent was shot dead less than a year later.

Bird travelled extensively, complaining that she only felt unwell when back in Britain, visiting Australia, Hawaii, India, Tibet, Persia, Kurdistan, Turkey, China, Korea, Morocco, Japan, Vietnam, Singapore and Malaysia. While in China, she became the first European woman to travel up the Yangtze River and was attacked by a mob that called her a "foreign devil" and trapped her in the top floor of a house, which they then set on fire. She was rescued at the last minute by some soldiers. She published at least 10 books about her travels, numerous articles and two books of photographs.

When she died, just shy of her 73rd birthday and a few months after a trip to Morocco, her saddle was sitting next to her bed, ready for her next adventure.

The edited account published here concerns one of Bird's most famous trips, to Korea in 1895, where she reported on the murder of Empress Myeongseong, known informally as Queen Min, at the hands of assassins sent by the Japanese government, who considered her to be an obstacle to their influence over the country.

As a newly risen power, Japan had gone to war with China to end its centuries-old suzerainty over Korea, and was determined to block any other power than it from dominating the country, which it thought of as "a dagger pointed at the heart of Japan". Tokyo also wanted the economic benefits of Korea's coal, iron ore and agriculture to help fuel its industries and feed its rapidly expanding population.

～

'THE QUEEN WAS DRAGGED BY HER HAIR, CUT, BEATEN AND STABBED REPEATEDLY, AND HER BODY BURNED IN KEROSENE OIL'

IN MAY 1895, a treaty of peace between China and Japan was signed at Shimonoseki: a heavy indemnity, the island of Formosa, and a great accession of prestige, being the gains of Japan. From thenceforward no power having interests in the Far East could afford to regard her as a *quantite negligeable*.

After travelling for some months in South and Mid China, and spending the summer in Japan, I arrived in Nagasaki in October 1895, to hear a rumour of the assassination of the Korean Queen, afterwards confirmed on board the *Suruga Maru* by Mr Sill, the American Minister, who was hurrying back to his post in Seoul in consequence of the disturbed state of affairs. I went up immediately from Chemulpo to the capital, where I was Mr Hillier's guest at the English Legation for two exciting months.

The native and foreign communities were naturally much excited by the tragedy at the Palace, and the treatment which the King was receiving. Count Inouye [Japan's ambassador to Korea], whose presence in Seoul always produced confidence, had left a month before, and had been succeeded by General Viscount Miura, a capable soldier without diplomatic experience.

In an interview which Count Inouye had with the Queen shortly before his departure, speaking of the ascendency of the [king's father] the Tai-Won-Kun, after the capture of the Palace by [the Japanese ambassador] Mr Otori in the previous July, Her Majesty said, "It is a matter of regret to me that the overtures made by me towards Japan were rejected. The Tai-Won-Kun, on the other hand, who showed his unfriendliness towards Japan, was assisted by the Japanese Minister to rise in power."

In the despatch in which Count Inouye reported this interview to his Government, he wrote:

"I gave as far as I could an explanation of these things to the Queen, and after so allaying her suspicions, I further explained that it was the true and sincere desire of the Emperor and Government of Japan to place the independence of Korea on a firm basis, and in the meantime to strengthen the Royal House of Korea. In the event of any member of the Royal Family or indeed any Korean therefore attempting treason against the Royal House, I gave the assurance that the Japanese Government would not fail to protect the Royal House even by force of arms, and so secure the safety of the kingdom. These remarks of mine seemed to have moved the King and Queen, and their anxiety for the future appeared to be much relieved."

The Korean sovereigns would naturally think themselves justified in relying on the promise so frankly given by one of the most distinguished of Japanese statesmen, whom they had learned to regard with confidence and respect, and it is clear to myself that when the fateful night came, a month later, their reliance on this assurance led them to omit certain possible precautions, and caused the Queen to neglect to make her escape at the first hint of danger.

When the well-known arrangement between Viscount Miura and the Tai-Won-Kun was ripe for execution, the Japanese Minister directed the Commandant of the Japanese battalion quartered in the barracks just outside the Palace gate to facilitate the Tai-Won-Kun's entry into the Palace by arranging the disposition of the Kun-ren-tai (Korean troops drilled by Japanese), and by calling out the Imperial force to support them. Miura also called upon two Japanese to collect their friends, go to Riong San on the Han, where the intriguing Prince was then living, and act as his bodyguard on his journey to the Palace. The Minister told them that on the success of the enterprise depended the eradication of the evils which had afflicted the kingdom for twenty years, and instigated them to despatch the Queen when they entered the Palace. One of Miura's agents then ordered the Japanese policemen who were off duty to put on civilian dress, provide themselves with swords, and accompany the conspirators to the Tai-Won-Kun's house.

At 3am on the morning of the 8th of October, they left Riong San escorting the Prince's palanquin, Mr Okamoto, to whom much had been entrusted, assembling the whole party when on the point of departure, and declaring to them that on entering the Palace the "Fox" should be dealt with according "as exigency might require". Then this procession, including ten Japanese who had dressed themselves in uniforms taken from ten captured Korean police, started for Seoul, more than three miles distant. Outside the "Gate of Staunch Loyalty", they were met by the Kun-ren-tai, and then waited for the arrival of the Japanese troops, after which they proceeded at a rapid pace to the Palace, entering it by the front gate, and after killing some of the Palace Guard, proceeded a quarter of a mile to the buildings occupied by the King and Queen, which have a narrow courtyard in front.

So far, I have followed the Hiroshima judgment in its statement of the facts of that morning, but when it has conducted the combined force to "the inner chambers" it concludes abruptly with a "not proven " in the case of all the accused. For the rest of the story, so far as it may interest my readers, I follow the statements of General Dye and Mr Sabatin of the King's Guard, and of certain official documents.

It is necessary here to go back upon various events which preceded the murder of Her Majesty. Trouble arose in October between the Kun-ren-tai and the Seoul police, resulting in the total defeat of the latter. The Kun-ren-tai,

numbering 1,000, were commanded by Colonel Hong, who
in 1882 had rescued the Queen from imminent danger, and
was trusted by the Royal Family. The Palace was in the
hands of the Old Guard under Colonel Hyon, who had
saved Her Majesty's life in 1884. In the first week of October,
the strength of this Guard was greatly reduced, useful
weapons were quietly withdrawn, and the ammunition was
removed.

ON THE NIGHT of the 7th the Kun-ren-tai, with their Japanese
instructors, marched and countermarched till they were
found on all sides of the Palace, causing some uneasiness
within. The alarm was given to General Dye [an American
military adviser to the king] and Mr Sabatin [a Russian
employed in the military service of Korea] early on the
morning of the 8th. These officers, looking through a chink
of the gate, saw a number of Japanese soldiers with fixed
bayonets standing there, who, on being asked what they
were doing, filed right and left out of the moonlight under
the shadow of the wall. Skulking under another part of the
wall were over 200 of the Kun-ren-tai. The two foreigners
were consulting as to the steps to be taken when heavy
sounds of battering came from the grand entrance gate,
followed by firing.

General Dye attempted to rally the Guard, but after five
or six volleys from the assailants they broke with such a
rush as to sweep the two foreigners past the King's house to
the gateway of the Queen's. No clear account has ever been
given of the events which followed. Colonel Hong, the
commander of the Kun-ren-tai, was cut down by a Japanese
officer at the great gate, and was afterwards mortally
wounded by eight bullets. The Kun-ren-tai swarmed into

the Palace from all directions, along with Japanese civilians armed with swords, who frantically demanded the where-abouts of the Queen, hauling the Palace ladies about by the hair to compel them to point out Her Majesty, rushing in and out of windows, throwing the ladies-in-waiting from the seven-feet-high verandah into the compound, cutting and kicking them, and brutally murdering two in the hope that they had thus secured their victim.

Japanese troops also entered the Palace, and formed in military order under the command of their officers round the small courtyard of the King's house and at its gate, protecting the assassins in their murderous work. Before this force of Japanese regulars arrived there was a flying rout of servants, runners, and Palace Guards rushing from every point of the vast enclosure in mad haste to get out of the gates. As the Japanese entered the building, the unfortunate King, hoping to divert their attention and give the Queen time to escape, came into a front room where he could be distinctly seen. Some of the Japanese assassins rushed in brandishing their swords, pulled His Majesty about, and beat and dragged about some of the Palace ladies by the hair in his presence. The Crown Prince, who was in an inner room, was seized, his hat torn off and broken, and he was pulled about by the hair and threatened with swords to make him show the way to the Queen, but he managed to reach the King, and they have never been separated since.

The whole affair did not occupy much more than an hour. The Crown Prince saw his mother rush down a passage followed by a Japanese with a sword, and there was a general rush of assassins for her sleeping apartments. In the upper storey the Crown Princess was found with several ladies, and she was dragged by the hair, cut with a sword, beaten, and thrown downstairs. Yi Kyong-jik, Minister of the

Royal Household, seems to have given the alarm, for the Queen was dressed and was preparing to run and hide herself. When the murderers rushed in, he stood with outstretched arms in front of Her Majesty, trying to protect her, furnishing them with the clue they wanted. They slashed off both his hands and inflicted other wounds, but he contrived to drag himself along the verandah into the King's presence, where he bled to death.

The Queen, flying from the assassins, was overtaken and stabbed, falling down as if dead, but one account says that, recovering a little, she asked if the Crown Prince, her idol, was safe, on which a Japanese jumped on her breast and stabbed her through and through with his sword.

Even then, though the nurse whom I formerly saw in attendance on her covered her face, it is not certain that she was dead, but the Japanese laid her on a plank, wrapped a silk quilt round her, and she was carried to a grove of pines in the adjacent deer park, where kerosene oil was poured over the body, which was surrounded by faggots and burned, only a few small bones escaping destruction.

THUS PERISHED, at the age of forty-four, by the hands of foreign assassins, instigated to their bloody work by the Minister of a friendly power, the clever, ambitious, intriguing, fascinating, and in many respects lovable Queen of Korea. In her lifetime Count Inouye, whose verdict for many reasons may be accepted, said, "Her Majesty has few equals among her countrymen for shrewdness and sagacity. In the art of conciliating her enemies and winning the confidence of her servants she has no equals."

A short time after daylight the Tai-Won-Kun issued two

proclamations, of which the following sentences are specimens : —

1st: "The hearts of the people dissolve through the presence in the Palace of a crowd of base fellows. So the National Grand Duke is returned to power to inaugurate changes, expel the base fellows, restore former laws, and vindicate the dignity of His Majesty."

2nd: " I have now entered the Palace to aid His Majesty, expel the low fellows, perfect that which will be a benefit, save the country, and introduce peace."

THE PALACE GATES were guarded by the mutinous Kun-ren-tai with fixed bayonets, who allowed a constant stream of Koreans to pass out, the remnants of the Old Palace Guard, who had thrown off their uniforms and hidden their arms, each man being seized and searched before his exit was permitted. Near the gate was a crimson pool marking the spot where Colonel Hong fell. Three of the Ministers were at once dismissed from their posts, some escaped, and many of the high officials sought safety in flight. Nearly everyone who was trusted by the King was removed, and several of the chief offices of State were filled by the nominee of the officers of the Kun-ren-tai who, later, when they did not find the Cabinet, which was chiefly of their own creation, sufficiently subservient, used to threaten it with drawn swords.

Viscount Miura arrived at the Palace at daylight, with Mr Sugimura, Secretary of the Japanese Legation (who had arranged the details of the plot), and a certain Japanese who had been seen by the King apparently leading the assassins, and actively participating in the bloody work, and had an audience of His Majesty, who was profoundly agitated. He signed three documents at their bidding, after which the

Japanese troops were withdrawn from the Palace, and the armed forces, and even the King's personal attendants, were placed under the orders of those who had been concerned in the attack. The Tai-Won-Kun was present at this audience.

During the day, all the Foreign Representatives had audiences of the King, who was much agitated, sobbed at intervals, and, believing the Queen to have escaped, was very solicitous about his own safety, as he was surrounded by assassins, the most unscrupulous of all being his own father. In violation of custom, he grasped the hands of the Representatives, and asked them to use their friendly offices to prevent further outrage and violence. He was anxious that the Kun-ren-tai should be replaced by Japanese troops. On the same afternoon, the Foreign Representatives met at the Japanese Legation to hear Viscount Miura's explanation of circumstances in which his countrymen were so seriously implicated.

Three days after the events in the Palace, and while the King and the general public believed the Queen to be alive, a so-called Royal Edict, a more infamous outrage on the Queen even than her brutal assassination, was published in the Official Gazette. The King on being asked to sign it refused, and said he would have his hands cut off rather, but it appeared as his decree, and bore the signatures of the Minister of the Household, the Prime Minister, and six other members of the Cabinet:

ROYAL EDICT

It is now thirty-two years since We ascended the throne, but Our ruling influence has not extended wide. The Queen Min introduced her relatives to the Court and placed them about Our person, whereby she made dull Our senses, exposed the people to extortion, put Our Government in disorder, selling offices and titles. Hence tyranny prevailed all over the country and robbers arose in all quarters. Under these circumstances the foundation of Our dynasty was in imminent peril. We knew the extreme of her wickedness, but could not dismiss and punish her because of helplessness and fear of her party.

We desire to stop and suppress her influence. In the twelfth moon of last year we took an oath at Our Ancestral Shrine that the Queen and her relatives and Ours should never again be allowed to interfere in State affairs. We hoped this would lead the Min faction to mend their ways. But the Queen did not give up her wickedness, but with her party aided a crowd of low fellows to rise up about Us and so managed as to prevent the Ministers of State from consulting Us. Moreover, they have forged Our signature to a decree to disband Our loyal soldiers, thereby instigating and raising a disturbance, and when it occurred she escaped. We have endeavoured to discover her whereabouts, but as she does not come forth and appear We are convinced that she is not only unfitted and unworthy of the Queen's rank, but also that her guilt is excessive and brimful. Therefore with her We may not succeed to the glory of the Royal Ancestry. So We hereby depose her from the rank of Queen and reduce her to the level of the lowest class.

Signed by

Yi Chai-myon, Minister of the Royal Household; Kim Hong-chip, Prime Minister; Kim Yun-sik, Minister of Foreign Affairs; Pak Chong-yang, Minister of Home Affairs; Shim Sang-hun, Minister of Finance; Cho Heui-yon, Minister of War; So Kwang-pom, Minister of Justice; So Kwang-pom, Minister of Education; Chong Pyong-ha, Vice-Minister of Agriculture and Commerce.

ON THE DAY following the issue of this fraudulent and infamous edict, another appeared in which Her Majesty, out of pity for the Crown Prince and as a reward for his deep devo-

tion to his father, was "raised" by the King to the rank of
Concubine of the First Order"!

The diplomats were harassed and anxious, and met
constantly to discuss the situation. Of course the state of
extreme tension was not caused solely by happenings in
Korea and their local consequences. For behind this well-
executed plot, and the diabolical murder of a defenceless
woman, lay a terrible suspicion, which gained in strength
every hour during the first few days after the tragedy till it
intensified into a certainty, of which people spoke as in
cipher, by hints alone, that other brains than Korean
planned the plot, that other than Korean hands took the
lives that were taken, that the sentries who guarded the
King's apartments while the deed of blood was being perpe-
trated wore other than Korean uniforms, and that other
than Korean bayonets gleamed in the shadow of the Palace
wall.

People spoke their suspicions cautiously, though the
evidence of General Dye and of Mr Sabatin pointed unmis-
takably in one direction. So early as the day after the affair,
the question which emerged was, "Is Viscount General
Miura criminally implicated or not?" It is needless to go into
particulars on this subject. Ten days after the tragedy at the
Palace, the Japanese Government, which was soon proved
innocent of any complicity in the affair, recalled and
arrested Viscount Miura, Sugimura, and Okamoto, Adviser
to the Korean War Department, who, some months later,
along with forty-five others, were placed on their trial before
the Japanese Court of First Instance at Hiroshima, and were
acquitted on the technical ground that there was "no sufficient evidence to prove that any of the accused actually
committed the crime originally meditated by them", this
crime, according to the judgment, being that two of the

accused, "at the instigation of Miura, decided to murder the Queen, and took steps by collecting accomplices... more than ten others were directed by these two persons to do away with the Queen".

Viscount Miura was replaced by Mr Komura, an able diplomatist, and shortly afterwards Count Inouye arrived, bearing the condolences of the Emperor of Japan to the unfortunate Korean King. A heavier blow to Japanese prestige and position as the leader of civilisation in the East could not have been struck, and the Government continues to deserve our sympathy on the occasion. For when the disavowal is forgotten, it will always be remembered that the murderous plot was arranged in the Japanese Legation, and that of the Japanese dressed as civilians and armed with swords and pistols, who were directly engaged in the outrages committed in the Palace, some were advisers to the Korean Government and in its pay, and others were Japanese policemen connected with the Japanese Legation - sixty persons in all, including those known as Soshi, and exclusive of the Japanese troops.

THE FOREIGN REPRESENTATIVES with one exception informed the Cabinet that until steps were taken to bring the assassins to justice, till the Kun-ren-tai Guard was removed from the Palace, and till the recently-introduced members of the Cabinet who were responsible for the outrages had been arraigned or at least removed from office, they declined to recognise any act of the Government, or to accept as authentic any order issued by it in the King's name. The prudence of this course became apparent later.

On 15th October, in an extra issue of the Official Gazette, it was announced "By Royal Command" that, as the position of Queen must not remain vacant for a day, proceedings for the choice of a bride were to begin at once.This was only one among the many insults which were heaped upon the Royal prisoner.

During the remainder of October and November, there was no improvement in affairs. The gloom was profound. Instead of Royal receptions and entertainments, the King, shaken by terror and in hourly dread of poison or assassination, was a close prisoner in a poor part of his own palace, in the hands of a Cabinet chiefly composed of men who were the tools of the mutinous soldiers who were practically his gaolers, compelled to put his seal to edicts which he loathed, the tool of men on whose hands the blood of his murdered Queen was hardly dry. Nothing could be more pitiable than the condition of the King and Crown Prince, each dreading that the other would be slain before his eyes, not daring to eat of any food prepared in the Palace, dreading to be separated, even for a few minutes, without an adherent whom they could trust, and with recent memories of infinite horror as food for contemplation.

General Dye, the American military adviser, an old and feeble man, slept near the Palace Library, and the American missionaries in twos took it in turns to watch with him. This was the only protection which the unfortunate sovereign possessed. He was also visited daily by the Foreign Representatives in turns, with the double object of ascertaining that he was alive and assuring him of their sympathy and interest. Food was supplied to him in a locked box from the Russian or US Legation, but so closely was he watched, that it was difficult to pass the key into his hand, and a hasty and very occasional whisper was the only communication he could succeed in making to these foreigners, who were his sole reliance. Undoubtedly from the first he hoped to escape either to the English or Russian Legation. At times he sobbed piteously and shook the hands of the foreigners, who made no attempt to conceal the sympathy they felt for the always courteous and kindly sovereign.

Entertainments among the foreigners ceased. The dismay was too profound and the mourning too real to permit even of the mild-gaieties of a Seoul winter. Every foreign lady, and especially Mrs Underwood, Her Majesty's medical attendant, and Mme Waeber, who had been an intimate friend, felt her death as a personal loss. Her Oriental unscrupulousness in politics was forgotten in the horror excited by the story of her end. Yet then and for some time afterwards people clung to the hope that she had escaped as on a former occasion and was in hiding. Among Koreans opinion was greatly concealed, for there were innumerable arrests, and no one knew when his turn might come, but it was believed that there was an earnest desire to liberate the King. A number of foreign warships lay at Chemulpo, and the British, Russian, and American Legations were guarded by marines.

Nearly a month after the assassination of the Queen, and when all hope of her escape had been abandoned, the condition of things was so serious under the rule of the new Cabinet, that an attempt was made by the Foreign Representatives to terminate it by urging on Count Inouye to disarm the Kun-ren-tai, and occupy the Palace with Japanese troops until the loyal soldiers had been drilled into an efficiency on which the King might rely for his personal safety. It will be seen from this proposal how completely the Japanese Government was exonerated from blame by the diplomatic agents of the Great Powers. This proposal was not received with cordial alacrity by Count Inouye, who felt that the step of an armed reoccupation of the Palace by the

Japanese, though with the object of securing the King's safety, would be liable to serious misconstruction, and might bring about very grave complications. Such an idea was only to be entertained if Japan received a distinct mandate from the Powers. The telegraph was set to work, due amount of consent to the arrangement was obtained, and when I left Seoul on a northern journey on November 7th, it was in the full belief that on reaching Pyongyang I should find a telegram announcing that this serious coup d'etat had been successfully accomplished in the presence of the Foreign Representatives. Japan, however, did not undertake the task, though urged to do so both by Count Inouye and Mr Komura, the new Representative, and the Kun-ren-tai remained in power, and the King a prisoner. Had the recommendation of the Foreign Representatives, among whom the Russian Representative was the most emphatic in urging the interference of Japan, been adopted, it is more than probable that the recent predominance of Russian influence in Korea would have been avoided. It is only fair to the Russian Government to state that it gave a distinct mandate to the Japanese to disarm the Kun-ren-tai and take charge of the King. The Japanese Government declined, and therefore is alone responsible for Russia's subsequent intervention.

During November, the dissatisfaction throughout Korea with the measures which were taken and proposed increased, and the position became so strained, owing to the demand of the Foreign Representatives and of all classes of Koreans that the occurrences of the 8th of October must be investigated, and that the fiction of the Queen being in hiding should be abandoned, that the Cabinet unwillingly recognised that something must be done. So on 26th November the Foreign Representatives were invited by the

King to the Palace, and the Prime Minister, in presence of His Majesty, who was profoundly agitated, produced a decree bearing the King's signature, dismissing the special nominees of the mutineers, the Ministers of War and Police, declaring that the so-called Edict degrading the Queen was set aside and treated as void from the beginning, and that she was reinstated in her former honours; that the occurrences of the 8th October were to be investigated by the Department of Justice, and that the guilty persons were to be tried and punished. The death of Her Majesty was announced at the same time.

At the conclusion of this audience, Mr Sill, the United States Minister, expressed to the King his profound satisfaction with the announcement. Mr Hillier followed by "congratulating His Majesty on these satisfactory steps, and hoped it would be the beginning of a time of peace and tranquillity, and relieve His Majesty from much anxiety". These good wishes were cordially endorsed by his colleagues.

The measures proposed by the King to reassert his lost authority and punish the conspirators promised very well, but were rendered abortive by a "loyal plot", which was formed by the Old Palace Guard and a number of Koreans, some of them by no means insignificant men. It had for its object the liberation of the sovereign and the substitution of loyal troops for the Kun-ren-tai. Though it ended in a fiasco two nights after this hopeful interview, its execution having been frustrated by premature disclosures, its results were disastrous, for it involved a number of prominent men, created grave suspicions, raised up a feeling of antagonism to foreigners, some of whom (American missionaries) were believed to be cognisant of the plot, if not actually accessories, and brought about a general confusion, from which, when I left Korea five weeks later, there was no prospect of escape. The King was a closer prisoner than ever; those surrounding him grew familiar and insolent; he lived in dread of assassination; and he had no more intercourse with foreigners, except with those who had an official right to enter the Palace, which they became increasingly unwilling to exercise.

It was with much regret that I left Seoul for a journey in the interior at this most exciting time, when every day brought fresh events and rumours, and a coup d'etat of great importance was believed to be impending; but I had very little time at my disposal before proceeding to Western China on a long-planned journey.

4

BERNAL DÍAZ - THE SLAUGHTER OF THE AZTECS, 1521

ernal Díaz del Castillo (c.1495-1584) was a Spanish soldier who took part in the conquest of Mexico and the destruction of the Aztec empire in 1521, under the leadership of Hernando Cortés.

Many years later, Díaz wrote a book detailing this invasion, called The True History of the Conquest of Mexico. *He describes some of the 119 battles in which he participated, culminating in the defeat of the Aztec civilisation, which was founded by the Mexica people and their allies in 1428 and, at its height, controlled five million people and huge swathes of present-day Mexico. Díaz's book describes the diverse people living there, and gives accounts of the human sacrifices, cannibalism and idolatry that they practised (it was central to Aztec belief that the return of human blood to the cosmos was vital to sustaining it). Tenochtitlán, their capital, was a city built on an island in Lake Texcoco, in what is today the historic centre of Mexico City. It was one of the largest cities in the world, with a population of 200,000-300,000, and boasted beautiful palaces, temples and public buildings, a botanical garden, two zoos and an aquarium.*

When Díaz and his fellow soldiers first saw it and its sister

cities, they were astonished. He wrote: "When we saw so many
cities and villages built in the water and other great towns on dry
land we were amazed on account of the great towers and cues
[temples] and buildings rising from the water, and all built of
masonry. Some of our soldiers even asked whether the things that
we saw were not a dream? I do not know how to describe it,
seeing things as we did that had never been heard of or seen
before, not even dreamed about."

Díaz, seemingly nothing more than a foot soldier, was one of
630 troops that Cortés had taken with him from Cuba on a
mission to colonise the mainland for Spain. Although vastly
outnumbered, the Spanish had several military advantages. They
were battle hardened after their conquests in the Caribbean, and
were extremely well armed. They had forged steel for their
swords, shields and armour. Their cross bows, guns and cannons
- which fired steel balls and balls fashioned from stone - were the
best available, giving them both a technological superiority over
an enemy that fought with spears, darts and rocks, as well as an
ability to attack at long range. They also had horses, the 16th-
century equivalent of tanks, giving them great mobility in open
battlefields.

Shrewdly, Cortés also made crucial alliances with indigenous
tribes who themselves had been conquered and subjugated by the
Aztecs, and who were forced to pay annual tributes to them.
Among the most important were the Tlascalan people.

During their first assault on the city, the Spanish had been
forced to retreat after Cortés had taken the Aztec ruler, Motecu-
zoma (or Montezuma, as Díaz styles him), prisoner and he subse-
quently died. The Spaniards and their Indian allies were forced to
fight their way out of the city, with heavy loss of life. Some
Spaniards died by drowning, loaded down with looted gold. They
retreated and eventually prepared for a second assault on
Tenochtitlán, with Cortés assembling a combined army of up to

100,000, the overwhelming majority of which were indigenous rather than Spanish. Through numerous subsequent battles and skirmishes, he captured various city-states around the lake shore and surrounding mountains, before turning to the Aztec capital.

Using boats constructed with parts salvaged from scuttled ships, Cortés blockaded and laid siege to Tenochtitlán for several months. Eventually, the Spanish-led army assaulted the city both by ship and the elevated causeways connecting it to the mainland. The attackers took heavy casualties, but the Aztecs were ultimately defeated. The city of Tenochtitlán was then deliberately destroyed. The Aztec king, Guatimotzin, was captured as he attempted to flee. Despite Cortés's assurances that he would be safe and allowed to continue as ruler, Guatimotzin was kept prisoner and tortured for a period of several years before he was finally executed in 1525.

This edited account from Díaz's book takes up the story as the Spanish conquistadors seek to fight their way to Tenochtitlán for the second time, against the enemy he calls the Mexicans.

'NEVER SINCE CREATION HAD A PEOPLE SUFFERED SO MUCH FROM HUNGER, THIRST AND WARFARE'

AS IT WAS impossible for our troops to advance upon the causeways without their flanks being secured on the water, the flotilla was formed into three divisions, and one of them attached to each of the three corps of our army; that is to say, four ships to Alvarado, six to De Oli, and two to Sandoval, making in all twelve. The thirteenth, being found to be too small, was ordered to be laid up, and her crew divided among the rest, as we had twenty very badly wounded already on board the ships. Alvarado now ordered us out upon the causeway, and placing two of the ships on each side, he thereby protected the flanks. We drove the enemy from several bridges and barricades, but after fighting during the whole day, we were obliged at night to retreat to our quarters, almost every man of us wounded by the showers of arrows and stones, which exceeded imagination; for we were attacked constantly by land by fresh troops bearing different devices, while from the terraces of the houses, the enemy commanded our ships. As we could not leave men to secure what we got in the day, at night the enemy repossessed the bridges, and put better defences on them. They deepened the water in some places, and in the shallow part they dug pits, and placed canoes in ambush, which they secured from the attacks of our vessels by palisades under the water. This was the manner in which they opposed us every day. The cavalry could do nothing; the enemy had built parapets across the causeways which they defended with long lances, and even had an attack been possible, the soldiers would not risk their horses, which at this time cost eight hundred crowns, and some more than one thousand - nor, indeed, were they to be had at any price.

When we arrived at night, we were employed in curing our wounds, and a soldier named Juan Catalan also healed them by charms and prayers, which, with the mercy of our Lord Jesus, recovered us very fast. But wounded or not, we were obliged to go against the enemy every day, as otherwise our companies would not have been twenty men strong. When our allies saw that the before mentioned soldier cured us by charms and prayers, all their wounded came to him, so that he had more business on his hands than he knew what to do with. Every day our ensign was disabled, not having it in his power to carry the colours, and defend himself. Corn we had sufficiency of, but we wanted refreshments for the wounded. What preserved us was the plant called "quilites", cherries while in season, and "tunas" or Indian figs.

THE ENEMY in the city rushed out on the signal being made from the top of the great temple of Tlaltelulco and these attacks were made every day, and repeated by fresh troops, who were formed and marched out in succession. Finding that we gained so little and lost so much, we resolved to change our plan of operations. There was on our causeway a small open place, where there were some buildings for religious worship; here we established a post, and lodged ourselves, though very badly; every shower of rain came in upon us, leaving our cavalry and Indian allies to secure our rear in Tacuba, from which place we were supplied with bread. From this time, as we advanced, we filled the water cuts which intersected the causeway, and levelled the houses which were on each side of it; for it was exceeding difficult to set them on fire, nor could the flames jump from one to another, on account of the water which was between them, and if we threw ourselves into the water to swim to a house, the enemy destroyed us from their terraces. We guarded every pass day and night as we gained it, and our method of keeping guard was as follows.

The company which was first for duty took it from sunset to midnight with forty men; the second company with the same number came on at midnight, and remained until two hours before daybreak, the first guard not quitting the post, but sleeping on the ground; this second guard watched the hours of lethargy, and after them came on the third company for the two hours until day, at which time, as those who were relieved did not quit the post, there were an hundred and twenty men at the guard. Sometimes our whole detachment remained under arms during the night, for our prisoners had informed us that it was the intention of the Mexicans, by a great effort, to force our post, as they knew that by so doing they would entirely disconcert the plans of the other two; and it was intended that the nine towns in and about the lake, including ours of Tacuba, together with Ezcapuzalco and Tenayuca, should make a joint effort, and attack us in the rear while the Mexicans attacked us in front. It was at the same time intended to carry off our luggage and bakery in Tacuba. This intelligence we immediately communicated to our cavalry, warning them and our allies to be well on their guard.

As we had been informed, so it happened: we were attacked for several nights in succession, from midnight to the break of day. The enemy sometimes came on with great noise, at others, they stole upon us in silence, but during the night their attacks were never made with so much resolution as in the day. We were, however, harassed to death with wounds, fatigues, wind, rain, and cold. The place where we were posted was now mud and water, and our miserable food of maize and herbs was all we had, but, as our officers said, such is the fortune of war! With all our sufferings, nothing effectual was gained: the parapets we threw down, or the ditches we filled up during the day, the enemy replaced in the ensuing night. What use was our cutting off their water, or closing their causeways against them, when they were supplied by canoes with whatever they wanted from the neighbouring towns on the lake? In order to prevent this, it was determined that two of our vessels should cruise during the night to intercept their canoes.

This was found to be the answer to a considerable degree, but still some escaped into the city.

THE MEXICANS HAD the boldness at this time to form a plan for the surprise of these vessels. They prepared thirty of their largest piraguas and concealed them among reeds, sending two or three canoes along the lake, as if conveying provisions, by way of a bait for our vessels. The Mexicans had also fixed piles of large timber below the water, in the direction which our ships were to be drawn in. The canoes being perceived by our people, two vessels sallied out upon them; the others appeared to take fright, and rowed towards the ambush, followed by our vessels, which as soon as they arrived near enough, were surrounded by the thirty piraguas. With the first discharge, they wounded every officer, soldier, and rower, on board; and the vessels could not stir on account of the piles of timber. The enemy continuing their attacks, killed a captain named Portilla; he was a gentleman who had served in Italy. Captain Pedro Barba of the crossbowmen also died of his wounds, and the vessels fell into their hands. They belonged to the principal division, which Cortés commanded; he was much exasperated, but in the course of a short time repaid them well in their own way.

Cortés and our other chiefs pursued their plan of advancing against the city. As they gained ground, they knocked down the houses, and with the materials filled up the ditches or canals which crossed the causeways; and our brave Tlascalan allies rendered us the greatest services, during the whole war. The Mexicans opposed our progress by breaking a bridge in the rear of their parapets and barricades, where the water was very deep, leaving one obvious pass as a decoy and in other parts, pitfalls under the water; they also made parapets on both sides of the breach, they placed palisades in the deep water where our vessels could approach, and they had canoes manned ready to sally out upon the signal given. When they had made these preparations they advanced against us in three bodies, one by the side of Tacuba, the other by the ruins of the houses which had been destroyed, and the third by the causeway, where they had made the works. Alvarado had brought part of his cavalry to our post, since the houses were destroyed. We repulsed the enemy on all sides, and one party of us having forced them from the work I have mentioned, crossed the water, up to our necks, at the pass they had left open, and followed them, until we came to a place where were large temples and towers of idols.

Here we were assailed by fresh troops from the houses and roofs, and those whom we pursued faced about and came against us. We were obliged to retreat, which we did with regularity, but when we came to the water, we found that the enemy in their canoes had got possession of the pass where we had crossed. We were therefore obliged to look for other places, but as they came pressing on us, we were at length compelled to throw ourselves into the lake and get over as we could. Those who were not able to swim fell into the pits; the enemy closed in upon them, wounded most, and took five of our soldiers alive. The vessels which came to our relief could not approach, being stuck among the palisades, and here they lost two soldiers. It was a wonder that we were not all destroyed in the pitfalls; a number of the enemy laid hands on me, but our Lord Jesus Christ gave me force to disengage my arm, and by dint of a good sword, I got free from them, though wounded, and arrived on the dry ground, where I fainted away, and remained senseless for a time. This was owing to my great exertions, and loss of blood. When this mob had their claws on me, I recommended myself to our Lord and his blessed mother, and they heard my prayer, glorified be they for all their mercies! One of our cavalry crossed the water with us this day; he and his horse were killed. Fortunately, the rest were with Alvarado in Tacuba; had they been with us they must have been all destroyed from the tops of the buildings, for the action took place as it were within the very city. After this success, the enemy kept us constantly employed during the day and night, by attacks upon our posts. Cortés was much dissatisfied at hearing of our defeat, which he considered was due to our neglect of his directions that the cuts across the causeways should be filled with timber and sods as we advanced.

IN THE SPACE of four days, and with the loss of six soldiers, we completely filled up this great aperture, and here we established our advanced post, the enemy having one opposite to us. Their method of keeping guard was this: they made a great fire in their front, which concealed them from our view, except when they came to renew the fire, as it was sometimes extinguished by the rains, which were at that season frequent and heavy. They kept profound silence on guard, nor was it ever interrupted except by their signals, which were given by a whistle. Our shot did no damage to them, for they fortified their post by a parapet and a new ditch. Having described the manner in which guard was kept on each side, I will now give an account of our daily employment. In the morning we marched against the enemy; after engaging them during the whole day, we retreated towards evening, covered with wounds, first clearing the causeway of our allies whose numbers embarrassed us, a circumstance the enemy were watchful to take advantage of, after which we fell back step by step, firing at the enemy as they advanced, and being flanked by the armed vessels, until we reached our post. When we arrived in our quarters, we sat down to our misery of maize cakes, herbs, and tunas, curing our wounds with oil, and remaining all night subject to constant alarms.

Cortés and his party were employed in the same manner, and his loss in killed and wounded was by this time become very considerable. He constantly sent out vessels at night to scour the lake, and one night they brought in to him some prisoners of consequence; from them he learned that the enemy had formed an ambush similar to their former one, of forty piraguas and the same number of canoes. Cortés then prepared six vessels, and sent them during the night, and with muffled oars, to a place of concealment within a quarter of a leagues' distance of that of the enemy. It must be observed that the bushes and tall reeds, and the water cuts at the edges of the lake, favored those deceptions. Early in the morning one of our vessels was sent as if in search of the Mexican canoes which went with provisions to the city, the prisoners being put on board it in order to point out the place where their flotilla was concealed. The enemy also played off the deception of loaded canoes to draw us thither, and these canoes pretending to endeavor to escape, rowed towards the ambush laid by their party; our vessel pursued them very near it, and then brought to, as if from apprehension. The enemy's flotilla perceiving that she did not advance, sallied out on her, those on board of her rowing towards that part where our ships were concealed. When they found that the enemy were brought to that point where we wished them to be, the crew fired two shots as a signal to our ambush, immediately on which the vessels pushed out, and falling on the enemy ran down several, and dispersed the rest, making a number of prisoners. This gave them enough of ambushes, nor did they from that time run across to Mexico so openly as before.

The people of the cities in the lake growing tired of this warfare, waited on Cortés at this time in order to make submission, declaring that they had been forced into hostility by the Mexicans. Cortés received them with affability, gave them assurances of protection according to their behaviour, and at the same time told them that he expected their assistance in the supply of boats and provisions, and in erecting barracks for the troops. This they promised readily, but performed very badly. Cortés had huts built for his detachment, but the rest remained exposed to the weather, a very severe duty in itself in that climate, as it rains continually during the months of June, July, and August.

OUR DETACHMENT PERSEVERED in filling up every ditch and canal as we proceeded with the materials of the houses which we destroyed and constantly gained temples, bridges, or houses which stood separate from each other, and were accessible by drawbridges only. To prevent jealousy, the companies took the working and covering parties alternately, and towards evening, when we drew off, the whole stood to their arms, and retreated, sending our Indian allies before us. The latter rendered us most important assistance in the working duty, both in pulling down the houses, and filling the apertures. Sandoval during this time was obliged to sustain constant attacks, and Cortés on his side attacked one of the outposts of the city, where the canal which crossed the causeway was too deep to be forded. The enemy had fortified it strongly, and defended it both by land and water. Cortés commanded the attack in person, and with success; but at night he was obliged to retire without filling the ditch, and with the loss of four Spaniards killed and above thirty wounded, for the pass was commanded from the terraces, and the palisades made in the water prevented the approach of the vessels.

Guatimotzin now determined to wear us out by continual efforts. Accordingly, on the twenty first of June, the anniversary of the day of our entry into Mexico, the enemy attacked us at every point with their whole force by land and water, at the hour of the second sleep, or of lethargy, that is two hours before day. The number fit for duty at our post was one hundred and twenty; our allies we had sent entirely off the causeway, and it was with our utmost efforts that we could resist the enemy; we at length however repulsed them from all our posts, but with the loss of many killed and wounded. Alvarado's detachment lost two soldiers on this occasion. The enemies' attacks were continued for two nights successively upon the different posts, and they afterwards concentrated their whole force in an assault upon ours, which took place at day break. This was the most desperate of all; if our allies had not been with us, we should have been lost. Our cavalry on this occasion saved our flanks, and we had considerable support from our ships. Eight of our soldiers were killed in this attack, and Alvarado was wounded; but we ultimately beat the enemy off, and also made four of their chiefs prisoners. I fear to tire my readers with this repetition of battles. For ninety-three days were we employed in the siege of this great and strong city, and every day and every night we were engaged with the enemy. Of course they must pardon what my duty as an historian compels me to relate; still were I to extend my narrative to include every action which took place, it would be almost endless.

CORTÉS, growing weary of delay, called a council of war, relative to a general assault upon the city. His plan was to march by the three causeways, and to endeavour to gain the great square, where, uniting our whole force, we should command all the streets leading to it. Upon this proposal there was a great difference of opinion, for many thought our present method of proceeding by filling the canals as we advanced, destroying the houses, and making a road with the materials, was preferable to that recommended by Cortés, whereby, in going into the heart of the city, we should become the besieged instead of being the besiegers, and fall exactly into the situation in which we had when obliged to retreat from Mexico. We should also, they said, be involved in greater difficulties than formerly, for the enemy would now bring their whole power by land and water upon us, so that we should have to contend with them in the city, on the lake, and all round it, without the possibility of retreat, which they could preclude by cutting the causeways.

When Cortés had heard the opinions of all, and the good reasons upon which they were founded, the result was that he gave orders for our whole force, together with our allies, to attack the city on the ensuing day, and to get possession of the great square.

On the next morning therefore, having heard mass, and recommending ourselves to God, our three detachments marched against the enemy's posts in their front. Those commanded by Cortés and Sandoval met with less violent opposition than that which fell to the lot of the division of Alvarado, to which I belonged. In our attack upon the first dyke, most of the Spaniards received wounds, one was killed, and above one thousand of our allies killed or wounded. Cortés at first bore down all before him, and having driven the enemy from a post where the water was very deep and the causeway very narrow, he was induced to pursue them in their retreat to the city, his Indian allies crowding close after the Spaniards. Cortés, with the whole of his division, now sure of victory, vigorously pursued the enemy, who from time to time faced about, to fly their arrows and lances at him; but all this was a mere stratagem on their part, to entice Cortés further into the city; and this object was entirely accomplished.

The wheel of fortune now suddenly turned against Cortés, and the joyous feelings of victory were changed into bitter mourning; for while he was eager in pursuit of the enemy, with every appearance of victory, it so happened that his officers never thought to fill up the large opening which they had crossed. The Mexicans had taken care to lessen the width of the causeway, which in some places was covered with water, and at others with a great depth of mud and mire. When the Mexicans saw that Cortés had passed the fatal opening without filling it up, their object was gained. An immense body of troops, with numbers of canoes, which lay concealed for this purpose in places where our brigantines could not get at them, now suddenly rushed forth from their hiding places, and fell upon this ill-fated division with incredible fierceness, accompanied by the most fearful yells. It was impossible for the men to make any stand against this overwhelming power, and nothing now remained for our men but to close their ranks firmly, and commence a retreat. But the enemy kept rushing on in such crowds, that our men, just as they had retreated as far back as the dangerous opening, gave up all further resistance, and fled precipitately. Cortés indeed strove to rally his men, and cried out to them, "Stand! Stand firm, gentlemen! Is it thus you turn your backs upon the enemy?" But all his commands were fruitless here, and every one strove to save his own life. Now the awful consequences of failing to fill up the opening in the causeway began to show themselves. In front of the narrow path, which the canoes had now broken down, the Mexicans wounded Cortés in the leg, took sixty Spaniards prisoners, and killed six horses. Several Mexican chiefs had already laid hands on our general, but with great exertion he tore himself from their grasp, and at the same moment the brave Christobal de Olea came to his assistance, cut down one of the Mexican chiefs who had seized hold of Cortés, and rescued his general, by cutting his way through the enemy sword in hand, assisted by another excellent soldier, called Lerma, But this heroic deed cost Olea his life, and Lerma was very nigh sharing a like fate. During this rescue of our general, several other of our men had by degrees hastened up to his assistance, who, though themselves covered with wounds, boldly risked their lives for Cortés. Antonio de Quinones, the captain of his guards, had likewise hastened up; they now succeeded in dragging Cortés out of the water, and, placing him on the back of a horse, he reached a place of safety. At this instant, his major domo, Christobal de Guzman, came up with another horse for him; but the Mexicans, who had become excessively daring, took him prisoner, and instantly carried him alive to Mexico. The enemy, in the meantime, pursued Cortes and his troops up to their very encampment, hooting and yelling most fearfully.

AFTER OUR DIVISION commanded by Alvarado made our first

attack, where we defeated the enemy, we advanced only to be met by fresh troops in great parade, bearing plumes of feathers, and devices on their standards. When we came near, they threw down before us five bleeding heads, crying out to us that they were those of Cortés and his officers, and that we should meet the same fate with our companions; they then marched up, and fighting us foot to foot, compelled us to retreat. We as usual called to our allies to clear the way for us, but there was no chance; the sight of the bloody heads had done its work effectively, not one of them remained on the causeway to help our retreat.

Before we arrived at our quarters, and while the enemy were pursuing us, we heard their shrill timbales, and the dismal sound of the great drum, from the top of the principal temple of the god of war, which overlooked the whole city. Its mournful noise was such as may be imagined the music of the infernal gods, and it might be heard at the distance of almost three leagues. They were then sacrificing the hearts of ten of our companions to their idols. Shortly after this, the king of Mexico's horn was blown, giving notice to his captains that they were then to take their enemies prisoners, or die in the attempt. It is impossible to describe the fury with which they closed upon us when they heard this signal. Though all is as perfect to my recollection as if passing before my eyes, it is utterly beyond my power to describe; all I can say is, it was God's will that we should escape from their hands, and get back in safety to our post. Praised be He for his mercies, now, and at all other times!

Our cavalry made several charges this day, but our great support was in two guns which raked the causeway, and were commanded by a gentleman named Pedro Moreno de Medrano, who always bore a high reputation as an officer, but whose services on this day were most important, for the whole causeway was crowded with the enemy. We were as yet ignorant of the fate of our other detachments. Sandoval was above half a league distant, and Cortés still farther. The melancholy fight of the remains of our countrymen, and the loss of one of our vessels, three of the soldiers of which the enemy had killed, impressed our minds with despair, and we thought this the last hour of our lives.

The vessel was afterwards recovered by that commanded by Captain Juan Xaramillo. Captain Juan de Limpias Caravajal, who now lives in La Puebla, a most gallant officer, had the honor of being the first who with his vessel broke through the enemies' palisades, totally losing his hearing, from this day, by excess of courage.

CORTÉS, most of whose soldiers had been killed, and what remained alive, wounded, was attacked in his quarters by a great body of the enemy, who threw over to him the heads of four of our companions, alleging them to be those of Alvarado, Sandoval, and others, in order to impress the soldiers of Cortés and our allies with the idea, that they had been equally successful against the other detachments. When Cortés beheld the horrid spectacle his heart sunk, but he kept up appearances, and ordering all to stand to their arms, made a front to the enemy. He then sent Andres de Tapia with three more mounted men to our quarters, in order to ascertain what the state of affairs was. On their way, they were attacked by many bodies of the enemy, whom the king of Mexico had placed upon a plan of intercepting our communications. On their arrival they found us engaged with the Mexican forces. They at that time concealed the losses of Cortés, stating it at no more than five and twenty.

It is now necessary to tell the story of Sandoval, who had

gone on victorious until the defeat of Cortés; after which the enemy turned on him, and in their first attack killed two soldiers and wounded all the rest, giving Sandoval himself three wounds, one of which was in the head. As they had done elsewhere, they threw before his troops six heads of their companions, recently taken off, threatening them with the same fate. Sandoval was not to be terrified; he warned his soldiers to preserve a good countenance, and seeing no hopes of success brought his division back to their quarters, with many wounded, but with the loss of only two.

Sandoval then, wounded as he was, leaving the command of his post to Captain Luis Marin, set out on horseback to have an interview with Cortés. As he went he was assailed by the enemy, but he arrived at the general's quarters, and addressing him in terms of surprise and condolence, asked him how this ill success had happened. "Son Sandoval," said Cortés, with tears in his eyes, "it is for my sins that this misfortune has befallen me; but the fault is with the treasurer Alderete, who was ordered by me to fill up the bad pass where the enemy threw us into confusion." The treasurer then exclaimed that it was with Cortés himself the fault lay, he having never given any such orders, but hurrying on his men after the enemy in their feigned retreat, crying, "Forward! Gentlemen, forward!" Cortés was also very much blamed for not having sent his allies out of the way early enough; however I will omit to detail any more of the conversation which passed at this time between Cortés and the treasurer, as it happened in the heat of anger and disappointment.

CORTÉS WAS AGREEABLY SURPRISED by the arrival of two of his vessels which he had given up for lost. Cortés desired

Sandoval to go to our quarters at Tacuba, as he thought that the weight of the enemy's attack would fall upon this position, and recommended that he should pay attention to our affairs, as he himself was at present unable to do so. Sandoval setting out, arrived at Tacuba about the hour of vespers. He also found us as Tapia had done, occupied in repelling the enemy, some of whom were attacking us by the causeway, others by that of the ruined houses. I was at this time together with others up to my waist in the water defending a vessel which was aground, and engaged with the enemy who were endeavouring to get possession of her. Just as Sandoval arrived however, by a great effort we got the vessel afloat, but with the loss of two of the crew killed, and every man on board wounded. The enemy now attacked us with more violence. Sandoval received a blow on the face with a stone, and called to us loudly to retreat; we not falling back as fast as he wished, he called again to us, asking if we wanted to have all the cavalry destroyed. We then retreated until we reached our post, during the time of which, our two guns, under the direction of Medrano, though they frequently swept the causeway, could not prevent the enemy from following us closely.

Here we were for a time at rest, and engaged in relating the events which had happened at each post, when on a sudden our ears were struck by the horrific sound of the great drum, the timbales, horns, and trumpets, in the temple of the war god. We all directed our eyes thither, and shocking to relate saw our unfortunate countrymen driven by force, cuffs, and bastinades, to the place where they were to be sacrificed, which bloody ceremony was accompanied by the mournful sound of all the instruments of the temple. They had brought the unfortunate victims to the flat summit of the temple, where there were the adoratories, put plumes upon their heads, and with a kind of fan in the hand of each, made them dance before their accursed idols. When they had done this, they laid them upon their backs, on the stone used for this purpose, where they cut out their hearts, alive, and having presented them, yet palpitating, to their god, they drew the bodies down by the feet, where they were taken by others of their priests. Let the reader think what were our sensations on this occasion. Oh heavenly God, we said to ourselves, do not suffer us to be sacrificed by these wretches! Do not suffer us to die so cruel a death! And then how shocking a reflection, that we were unable to relieve our poor friends who were thus murdered before our eyes!

At this moment the enemy assailed our post in great force, reviling us and saying their gods had promised us all to them. Our Indian allies sunk under the dreadful ideas they expressed, when they threw among them also some of the mangled remains of their horrid feats, other parts being sent round all the neighbouring districts, as a triumphant memorial. We still, however, maintained possession of our post, one half of our cavalry being on the causeway and the other half in the town.

OUR NEW ALLIES on the lake had suffered considerably by the enemy, having lost half their canoes, but they continued firm to us, from animosity to them, or contented themselves with being mere lookers on, and did not molest us. Cortés, in consequence of our losses, ordered a cessation of attacks, which lasted for four days, during which we did not quit our posts, having lost near eighty men, and seven horses, in the engagement. The enemy also gained ground on us, and made new ditches and water cuts, but we had a very deep and defensible one in front of our quarters. Sandoval and Tapia on their return to the general, reported to him the valiant manner in which our soldiers had been behaving when they arrived at our post; Sandoval also mentioned me particularly, and said those things in my commendation, which, exclusive of the facts being known to our whole army, would not be proper to repeat of myself.

During this cessation, our whole force of infantry kept guard on the causeway at night, flanked by the brigantines, one half of the cavalry patrolling in Tacuba, the other half on the causeway. In the morning we prepared to receive the enemy, who every day continued sacrificing our poor companions, and when they attacked, reviled us, saying that our flesh was too bitter to be eaten, and truly it seems that such a miracle was wrought. For five days, the enemy continued their assaults, being promised our destruction by their gods, within the space of eight days; but their gods, as it appears to me, were perverse and treacherous to them, not permitting them to think of peace, and thus leading them to ruin. This language however, and the last menace in particular, had such an effect upon our allies, together with the bad appearance of our affairs, that they almost entirely deserted us in the course of a night. The only one who remained with Cortés, was Suchel, otherwise Don Carlos, brother of Fernando lord of Tezcuco. He was a man of great bravery. His friends who stayed by him amounted to about forty. With Sandoval remained the chief of Guaxocingo, with about fifty, and in ours the brave Chichimecatecle, the two sons of our friend D. Lorenzo de Vargas, and about eighty Tlascalans. Questioned as to the flight of their countrymen, they said that the gods of the Mexicans had predicted our destruction; that they saw us all wounded, and many killed, that their own losses were more than 1,200 killed, and that the younger Xicotenga had from the first foretold that we should be all put to death; and therefore, considering us as lost, their countrymen had given up on us.

Cortés, though he thought much of what they said was too true, put on a cheerful appearance, ridiculed the predictions of the enemy, and assured them that all would end well. He thereby was fortunate enough to induce the few who yet remained to stay with us to the last. The Indian Don Carlos, a brave and wise man, now pointed out to Cortés the erroneous manner in which the general had acted, and also the situation the enemy was in, advising him not to suffer his troops to fight. "Cut off their provisions and water," he said. "There are in Mexico so many warriors, how can they subsist? Their provisions must at some time be expended, the water which they get from the wells is salt, and they have no resource but from the frequent rains. Fight them by hunger and thirst, and do not throw away your own force." Cortés embraced D. Carlos for his advice; not that the same had not occurred to many of us before, but we were too impatient.

Cortés began by sending orders to all the detachments to remain in their quarters for the next three days. As the enemy were so strong upon the lake, we always sent out two vessels in company; they had now acquired the method of breaking through the palisades by the force of oars and sails, when there was a good wind. Thus we were masters of the lake, and also of all the houses which were at any little distance from the city. This slackened the triumphs of the Mexicans. As our vessels broke through the enemy's palisades, they could flank us while we carried on our work, filling the ditches in our front. This we effected at all our posts in the space of four days, Cortés himself carrying the beams and earth.

During each night of this period, the enemy continued beating their accursed drum in the great temple; nothing can equal the dismal impression its sound conveyed. They were then in the execution of their infernal ceremonies; the whole place was illuminated, and their shrieks at certain intervals pierced the air. For ten nights, they were thus employed in putting to death our unfortunate companions; Christobal de Guzman was the last sacrificed; he was in their hands eighteen days; we were informed of this by some of our prisoners, and for every sacrifice, we were told that their war god renewed to them the promise of victory. The enemy at times during the foregoing period brought our own crossbows against us, and made the unfortunate prisoners shoot them; but our post derived its safety from the excellent management of the two guns under P. M. Medrano, and we still advanced, gaining every day a bridge or a parapet. Our vessels also continually intercepted their canoes loaded with provisions and water, also those which were employed in procuring a nutritive substance which when dry resembles cheese, and is found at the bottom of the lake.

In this manner, twelve or thirteen days had now passed, and our lives therefore exceeded the date allowed them by the prediction of the Mexican priests. This gave our allies courage, and in compliance with the requisition of our steady friend Suchel, two thousand warriors from Tezcuco returned to us. There came with them Captain Pedro Sanchez Farfan, and Anthonio de Villaroel, afterwards married to La Ojeda, who had been left behind in Tezcuco. Many bodies also of our Tlascalan and other allies arrived about the same time. Cortés having summoned their chiefs, made them a speech, partly of reprimand and partly of hopes and promises, concluding it with an admonition to them not to put to death any of the Mexicans, as it was his wish to negotiate for peace.

The heavy rains at this season of the year were much in our favor, the enemy always relaxing their exertions when they came on. We had now advanced considerably into the city with each of the three attacks; we had also reached the fountains of brackish water, which we totally destroyed, and the cavalry could act through the whole space which we had gained, as it was our care to make it level for them.

OUR GENERAL THOUGHT the present a good juncture to offer peace to the Mexicans; he therefore proposed to three of his principal prisoners to go with a message to their king, Guatimotzin, but they declined it, alleging that he would certainly put them to death. At length, however, he prevailed with them to carry his proposal, which was to this purport. That from the affection he bore to all the family of the great Montezuma, in order also to prevent the destruction of that great city, and the loss of lives, he was willing to agree a peace treaty. He reminded Guatimotzin that his troops and people were cut off from provisions and water, and that all those nations which had formerly been the vassals of Mexico were now the allies of the Spaniards; with many more strong arguments to the same purpose, which the ambassadors very well understood. Previous to their going, they desired that the general would provide them with a letter, under which authority they waited on the monarch, sobbing and wailing bitterly, as knowing the danger which attended their mission.

At first, Guatimotzin and his chiefs appeared enraged, but the moderation of his disposition prevailed, and he resolved to call a council composed of the princes, chiefs and priests of the city. Guatimotzin started by expressing his own inclination to come into terms, exposing the inefficacy of their resistance, the desertion of their allies, and the distress of the people. The priests took the opposite opinion. They represented the conduct of the Spaniards from the first, their treatment of his uncle, the great Montezuma, of Cacamatzin, and of various other princes as soon as they had got them in their power; also the death of the two sons of Montezuma, which they laid to their charge, the destruction and waste of the wealth of Mexico, and the marks of slavery with which they had branded other nations. They reminded him of his own martial fame and conduct, of the insidiousness of Cortés and his offers, and the promises of victory they had obtained from their gods. Guatimotzin then expressed his determination to fight to the last man and gave orders to spare the provisions as much as possible, to sink wells in various places, and to endeavour to obtain supplies by night.

Our army remained quietly at their posts for two days, expecting the answer from Mexico. We were then attacked at all points by great bodies of the enemy, who fell on us like lions, closing upon and endeavouring to seize us in their hands, whenever the horn of Guatimotzin was sounded. For seven days were we thus engaged, watching in a body during the night, at day break going into action, fighting during the day, and in the evening retiring to console ourselves with our misery of maize cakes, *agi* or pepper, tunas, and herbs. Our offer of peace only served as new matter for the enemy to revile us on, reproaching us as cowards, saying that peace was for women and arms for men.

IT HAS BEEN MENTIONED that the wretched remains of our countrymen were sent round to different provinces, to summon and encourage them to come to the aid of the Mexicans. In consequence, a force assembled from Matalzingo, Malinalco, and other places at the distance of eight leagues from Mexico, to fall on our rear, while the enemy from the city attacked us in front. When they had assembled, they began to commit outrages upon the country between them and us, seizing the children in order to sacrifice them. Complaints of this coming to Cortés, he detached Andres de Tapia with twenty cavalry and one hundred infantry against the enemy. This officer executed his mission completely, driving them back to their own country with losses.

Cortés then sent Sandoval to assist the people of the district called by us Cuernabaca, who were attacked in the same manner. There is much to say in respect to this expedition; too much indeed to be able to do justice to it without going into the details; suffice it that it was more peaceable than warlike, and had the happiest effect for us, Sandoval returned accompanied by two chiefs of the nation he had marched against. His return was very sudden, in order to protect our posts, which were in a most perilous way; for this draft had dismantled them, as he had with him every man really fit for duty, being twenty cavalry and eighty infantry. However, his expedition saved both our allies and us.

Cortés now again sent an envoy to Guatimotzin, saying he had his Monarch's orders to save if possible that fine city; he reminded Guatimotzin of the distress of the wretched people, and to convince him that he had no hope from his allies, he sent the message by the two chiefs who accompanied Sandoval. The Mexican monarch returned no answer, except ordering the ambassadors immediately to quit the city. The enemy now increased every day the fury of their attacks; their expressions were, "Tenitoz re de Casilla! Tenitoz Axaca?" which meant, "What says the king of Castille? What does he now?" We still continued advancing towards the heart of the city, and observed that notwithstanding the rage with which they assailed us, for it seemed as if they wished to meet their deaths, there was not so much movement among them as formerly, nor did they so busily employ themselves in opening the ditches. We also had cause for reflection of a less pleasant nature which was that our powder was almost reduced to nothing.

At this moment, most fortunately, there arrived at the port of Villa Rica, a vessel with soldiers and ordnance stores, one of an armament fitted out by the Licentiate Lucas Vasquez de Aillon, which had been destroyed or dispersed near the Islands of Florida. The relief and reinforcement were immediately forwarded to Cortés, by his lieutenant, Rangel.

IT WAS NOW DETERMINED by Cortés and all the army to push for the great place or Tlaltelulco of the city, on account of the principal temples and strong buildings being there. Each of our detachments therefore advanced for the purpose. Cortés got possession of a small square at which were some temples; in those temples were beams whereon were placed the heads of many of our soldiers; their hair and beards had much grown; I could not have believed it had I not seen it with my own eyes in three days after, when our party had advanced near enough to get a view of them, after having filled two canals. I recognised the features of three of our friends, and the tears came into my eyes at the sight. In twelve days, they were all buried by us in that which is now named the church of the martyrs.

The detachment of Alvarado continued to advance, and after an engagement of two hours forced the enemy from their barricades in the great square. The cavalry now rendered good service in the open space, and the enemy were driven before us into the temple of the war god.

Alvarado divided his forces into three bodies, and while he occupied the attention of the enemy with two, he ordered the third, commanded by Gutierre de Badajoz, to drive them from, and take possession of the great temple. The enemy, headed by their priests, occupied the adoratories of their idols, and repulsed our troops, driving them down the steps; which being observed by Alvarado, he then sent us to support them, and on our arrival, having ascended to the top, we completely drove the enemy from that post; having done which, we set fire to the images of their false gods, and planted our standard on the summit of the temple. The view of this signal of victory rejoiced Cortés, who would have joined us, but he had it not in his power. He was then distant a quarter of a league, and had many ditches to fill as he advanced. In four days from this time, both he and Sandoval had worked their way to us, and the communications to the three posts were opened through the centre of the city of Mexico. This attack upon the temple was truly perilous; the edifice was very lofty, the enemy numerous and they continued to engage us on the flat ground at the summit, from the time that we had set fire to the idols and their adoratories, until night. The royal palaces were now levelled to the ground, Guatimotzin and his troops having retired to a quarter of the city more distant from the centre, towards the lake.

Still they attacked us in the day, and at night pursued us

to our quarters, and thus time passed, and no proposition was made concerning peace. Our chiefs then proposed an ambush. Thirty cavalry and one hundred infantry of the prime of our army, together with one thousand Tlascalans were concealed in some large houses which had belonged to a nobleman of the city. This was done during the night. Cortés with the rest of his troops, in the morning went to attack a position at a bridge, which Guatimotzin had ordered to be supported by a large force. Cortés after his first attack retreated, drawing the enemy after him, by the buildings where our troops were concealed. At the proper moment he fired two shots close together as a signal to us; we sallied out, and the enemy being enclosed between us, our allies, and the party of Cortés which faced about, a dreadful havoc was made of them, and from that time they no more annoyed us in our retreat. Another trap was also laid for them by Alvarado, but not with the same success; I was not present at it, being ordered by Cortés to do duty for that time with his party.

From our quarters, we had to march above half a league to meet the enemy; we now therefore left that post altogether, and lodged ourselves in the great square, or Tlaltelulco. Here we were for three days without doing anything worth mentioning: we also abstained from destroying any more of the city, in the hopes of peace.

Cortés at this time sent to Guatimotzin requesting him to surrender, under the strongest assurances of enjoying the plentitude of power and honors. He accompanied this offer with as handsome a present as his situation permitted, of provisions, bread, fowls, fruit, and game.

Guatimotzin, as he was advised to do by those whom he consulted, dissimulated, and seemed inclined to a pacification. He sent four of his principal nobles, with a promise to come to an interview with Cortés in three days. But this was all feigned; he employed the time in fortifying his quarter of the town, and making preparations to attack us. He also endeavoured to amuse us by sending a second ambassador, but we were now advised of his schemes. In fact, from what he was told by those about him, and from the example of his uncle Montezuma, he was afraid to trust himself in our hands. But the mask was soon thrown off; we were attacked by great bodies of the enemy, with such violence that it appeared as if all was beginning anew. Having been rather taken by surprise, they did us at first some mischief, killing one soldier and two horses, but in the end we sent them back with very little to boast of. Cortés ordered his troops now to proceed against that part of the city where the quarters of Guatimotzin were; accordingly we began upon our former system, and gained ground as we had before done elsewhere. When the king perceived this, he desired an interview with Cortés, on the side of a large canal which was to separate them. To this Cortés readily assented, and it was to take place on the ensuing morning. Cortés attended, but Guatimotzin never appeared; instead of which he sent several of his principal nobility, who said that the king did not think it proper to come, from an apprehension that we might shoot him during the parley. Cortés then engaged by the most solemn oaths not to do him any injury whatever, but it was of no effect. A ridiculous farce was played here: two of the nobility who attended on, the part of Guatimotzin, took out of a sack, bread, a fowl, and cherries, which they began to eat, in order to try to impress the Spaniards with an idea that they were not in want. Cortés, seeing the manner in which he was treated, sent back an hostile message and retired; after this we were left unmolested for four or five days. During this time, numbers of wretched

Indians, reduced by famine, surrounded our quarters every night. Cortés pitied their miserable situation, and hoping that it might induce the enemy to come into terms of accommodation, ordered the cessation of hostilities to be strictly adhered to; but no overture of the kind was made.

THERE WAS in the army of Cortés a soldier who boasted of having served in Italy, and of the great battles which he had seen there. His name was Sotelo, and he was a native of Seville. This man was eternally talking of the wonderful military machines which he knew the art of constructing, and how he could make a stone engine which should in two days destroy that whole quarter of the city where Guatimotzin had retreated. He told Cortés so many fine things of this kind, that he persuaded him into a trial of his experiments, lime, stone and timber being brought, according to his desire; the carpenters were also set to work, two strong cables were made, and stones the size of a bushel were prepared. The machinery was now all ready, the stone which was to be ejected was put in its place, and the whole apparatus was aimed at the quarters of Guatimotzin. But instead of taking that direction, the stone flew up vertically into the air, and returned exactly into the place from whence it had been launched. Cortés was enraged and ashamed: he reproached the soldier, and ordered the machinery to be taken down; but still it continued to be the joke of the army.

Cortés now gave orders to Sandoval, to go with the flotilla against that part or nook of the city whither Guatimotzin had retired, cautioning him at the same time not to kill or injure any Mexican, unless he was attacked, nor even then to do more than was absolutely necessary for his own defence, but to level all the houses, and the many advanced works which the enemy had made in the lake. Cortés ascended then into the great temple, with several of his officers and soldiers, to observe the movements of his fleet. When Sandoval approached the quarters of Guatimotzin, that prince, who had great apprehensions of being made prisoner, availed himself of the preparations which he had made for his escape, and embarking himself, his family, his courtiers, and officers, with their most valuable effects, on board fifty large piraguas, the whole body set off for the mainland, as did all his nobility and chiefs in various directions. Sandoval, who was at this time occupied in making his way by tearing down the houses, received immediate notice of the flight of Guatimotzin. He instantly set out in the pursuit, giving orders that no injury or insult should be offered, but that each should keep a steady eye upon the royal vessel, and do his utmost to get possession of it. He particularly directed Garci Holguin, his intimate friend, and captain of the quickest vessel of the fleet, to make for that part of the shore where Guatimotzin was most likely to go.

This officer followed his instructions, and falling in with the vessels, from certain particulars in its appearance, structure and awning, he ascertained that which the king was on board of. He made signs to the people in it to bring to, but without effect; he then ordered his crossbow-men and musketeers to present, upon which Guatimotzin called out to them not to shoot, and approaching the vessel, acknowledged himself for what he was, declaring his readiness to submit, and go with them to their general, but requesting that his queen, his children, and attendants should remain unmolested. Holguin received him with the greatest respect, together with his queen, and twenty of his nobility. He seated them on the poop of his ship, and provided refreshments for them, commanding that the piraguas which carried the king's effects, should follow untouched.

Sandoval at this moment made a signal for the flotilla to close up to him, and perceived that Guatimotzin was prisoner to Holguin, who was taking him to Cortés. Upon this he ordered his rowers to exert their utmost to bring him up to Holguin's vessel, and having arrived by the side of it, he demanded Guatimotzin to be delivered to him as general of the whole force; but Holguin refused, alleging that he had no claim whatever. A vessel which went to carry the intelligence of the great event, brought also to Cortés who was then on the summit of the great temple in Tlaltelulco, very near the part of the lake where Guatimotzin was captured, an account of the dispute between his officers. Cortés instantly dispatched Captain Luis Marin and Francisco de Lugo, to bring the whole party together to his quarters, and thus to stop all the arguing; but he enjoined them not to omit treating Guatimotzin and his queen with the greatest respect. During the interval, he prepared a table with refreshments, to receive his prisoners. As soon as they appeared, he went forward to meet them, and embracing Guatimotzin, treated him and all his attendants with every mark of respect. The unfortunate monarch, with tears in his eyes, and sinking under affliction, then addressed him in the following words: "Malintzin! I have done that which was my duty in the defence of my kingdom and people; my efforts have failed, and being now brought by force a prisoner in your hands, draw that poinard from your side, and stab me to the heart."

CORTÉS EMBRACED HIM, and used every expression to comfort him, by assurances that he held him in high estimation for the valour and firmness he had shown, and that he had required a submission from him and the people at the time that they could no longer reasonably hope for success, in order to prevent further destruction; but that was all past, and no more to be thought of; he should continue to reign over the people, as he had done before. Cortés then enquired after his queen, to which Guatimotzin replied, that in consequence of the compliance of Sandoval with his request, she and her women remained in the piraguas, until Cortés should decide as to their fate. The general then caused them to be sent for, and treated them in the best manner his situation afforded. The evening was drawing on, and it appeared likely to rain; he therefore sent the whole royal family to Cuyoacan, under the care of Sandoval. The rest of the troops then returned to their former quarters; we to ours at Tacuba, and Cortés, proceeding to Cuyoacan, took the command there, sending Sandoval to resume his station at Tepeaquilla. Thus was the siege of Mexico brought to a conclusion by the capture of Guatimotzin and his chiefs, on the thirteenth of August, at the hour of vespers, being the day of St Hyppolitus, in the year of our Lord one thousand five hundred and twenty one. Glorified be our Lord Jesus Christ, and our lady the Holy Virgin Mary his blessed mother, Amen!

In the night after Guatimotzin was made prisoner, there was the greatest tempest of rain, thunder, and lightning, especially about midnight, that ever was known; but all the soldiers were as deaf to it as if they had been for an hour in a steeple, with the bells ringing about their ears. This was owing to the continual noise of the enemy for the past ninety-three days; some preparing their troops and bringing them on, shouting, calling, and whistling, as signals to attack us on the causeway; others in the canoes coming to attack our vessels; some again at work upon their palisades, or opening the ditches and water cuts, and making stone parapets, or preparing their magazines of darts and arms, and the women supplying the flingers with their ammunition. Then from the temples and adoratories of their accursed idols, the timbales and horns, and the mournful sound of their great drum, and other dismal noises, were incessantly assailing our ears, so that day or night we could hardly hear each other speak. But these dins immediately ceased on the capture of Guatimotzin.

GUATIMOTZIN WAS of a noble appearance both in person and countenance; his features were rather large, and cheerful, with lively eyes. His age was about twenty three or four years, and his complexion very fair for an Indian. His queen, the niece of Montezuma, was young, and very handsome.

What I am going to mention is truth, and I swear and say amen to it. I have read of the destruction of Jerusalem, but I cannot conceive that the mortality there exceeded this of Mexico; for all the people from the distant provinces which belonged to this empire had concentrated themselves here, where they mostly died. The streets, the squares, the houses, and the courtyards of the Tlaltelulco were covered with dead bodies; we could not step without treading on them; the lake and canals were filled with them, and the stench was intolerable. For this reason, our troops immediately after the capture of the royal family retired to their former quarters. Cortes himself was for some time ill from the effect of it.

The vessels were now the best situation, those on board carrying away all the plunder, for they had access to houses in the water which were not in our reach. They also found what the Mexicans had concealed in the reeds, and on the borders of the lake, and intercepted that which was carried out of our reach by water. We on land gained nothing but honor and wounds. The wealth our navy got was much more than we could guess at; Guatimotzin and all his chiefs declaring, when enquiry was made as to the public treasure, that it had mostly fallen into their hands.

To return to the state of Mexico. Guatimotzin now requested of Cortes, that permission should be given to clear the city entirely of the inhabitants, in order to purify it, and restore its salubrity. Accordingly they were ordered to remove to the neighbouring towns, and for three days and three nights, all the causeways were full, from one end to the other, of men, women, and children, so weak and sickly, squalid and dirty, and pestilential that it was misery to behold them. When all those who were able had quitted the city, we went to examine the state of it. The streets, courts, and houses were covered with dead bodies, and some miserable wretches were creeping about, in the different stages of the most offensive disorders, the consequences of famine and improper food. The ground was all broken up to get at the roots of such vegetation as it afforded, and the trees were stripped of their bark. There was no fresh water in the town. During all their distress, however, though their constant practice was to feast on those they took prisoner, no instance occurred of their having preyed on each other; and certainly never existed since the creation a people which suffered so much from hunger, thirst, and warfare.

5

AMERIGO VESPUCCI - ENCOUNTERS
WITH BRAZILIAN CANNIBALS, 1501

*A*merigo Vespucci (1454-1512) was a merchant from Florence who, at the age of almost 50, decided to retire from business and go to sea. While living and working in Cadiz and Seville, part of his work had been to deliver provisions for explorers such as Columbus (who was four years his senior) and to ensure that an order from the crown for twelve 900-ton ships was fulfilled, so he was well connected with admirals, explorers and royalty.

At the invitation of King Manuel I of Portugal, Vespucci participated as an observer in several voyages (the exact number is a matter of historical dispute) that visited the east coast of South America between 1499 and 1502, discovering that the continent extended much farther south than was previously thought.

In September 1504, he wrote an account of these voyages. In 1507, a German cartographer, Martin Waldseemüller, produced a world map naming the new continent America after the feminine Latin version of Vespucci's first name, which is Americus. Vespucci has also been hailed by him as "the discoverer and conqueror of Brazilian land".

The edited extract published here is taken from a letter

written by Vespucci to an old friend, a nobleman in Florence, and concerns what he termed his third voyage, which was was led by Captain General Goncalo Coelho. Departing from Lisbon, the fleet sailed first to Cape Verde, then to Brazil, reaching Guanabara Bay on New Year's Day 1502 and naming it Rio de Janeiro (River of January), before possibly reaching as far south as Patagonia and South Georgia.

'THE WOMEN CUT THE CHRISTIAN INTO BITS, ROASTED HIM ON A GREAT FIRE BEFORE OUR EYES, AND THEN ATE HIM'

MAGNIFICENT LORD

I know not how there came into the thoughts of the Most Serene King Don Manuel of Portugal the wish to have my services. But being at Seville, without any thought of going to Portugal, a messenger came to me with a letter from the Royal Crown, in which I was asked to come to Lisbon, to confer with his Highness, who promised to show me favour.

When I was presented to that King, he showed his satisfaction that I had come, and asked me to go in company with three of his ships that were ready to depart for the discovery of new lands. As the request of a king is a command, I had to consent to whatever he asked. We sailed from Lisbon, three ships in company, on the 10th day of May 1501, and took our route directly for the Island of Great Canary: and we passed in sight of it without halting. From hence we went skirting along the coast of Africa on the west side, on which coast we exercised our fishing-skill on a kind of fish which are called Parchi.

We made for the coast of Ethiopia, to a port which is called Besechicce, where we remained for 11 days, taking in water and firewood, because my intention was to make our way southerly through the Atlantic gulf. We left this port, and navigated south-westwardly, taking one quarter by south, until after a course of 67 days we anchored at a land which was 700 leagues to the south-west of the said port: and in those 67 days, we had the worst weather that ever any seafarer had, being struck by numerous storm-showers, whirlwinds, and tempests.

It pleased God to show us a new land on the 17th of August, and we anchored at a distance of half a league, and got our boats out. We then went to see the land, whether it was inhabited, and what it was like. We found that it was inhabited by people who were worse than animals. But your Magnificence must understand that we did not see them at first, though we were convinced that the country was inhabited, by many signs observed by us. We took possession for that Most Serene King; and found the land to be very pleasant and fertile, and of good appearance. It was five degrees to the south of the equinoctial line.

We went back to the ships, and as we were in great want of wood and water, we determined, next day, to return to the shore, with the object of obtaining what we wanted. Being on shore, we saw some people at the top of a hill, who were looking at us, but without showing any intention of coming down. They were naked, and of the same colour and form as others we had seen. We tried to induce them to come and speak with us, but did not succeed, as they would not trust us. Seeing their obstinacy, and it being late, we returned on board, leaving many bells and mirrors on shore, and other things in their sight. As soon as we were at some distance on the sea, they came down from the hill, and showed themselves to be much astonished at the things we had left. On that day, we were only able to obtain water.

Next morning, we saw from the ship that the people on shore had made a great smoke, and thinking it was a signal to us, we went on shore, where we found that many people had come, but they still kept at a distance from us. They made signs to us that we should come inland with them. Two of our Christians were, therefore, sent to ask their captain for leave to go with them a short distance inland, to see what kind of people they were, and if they had any riches, spices, or drugs. The captain was content, so they got together many things for barter, and departed from us, with instructions that they should not be more than five days, as we would only wait that long for them. So they set out on their road inland, and we returned to the ships to wait for them. Nearly every day people came to the beach, but they would not speak with us. On the seventh day we went on shore, and found that the men had sent many of their women to speak with us.

Seeing that they were not reassured, we arranged to send to them one of our people, who was a very agile and valiant youth. To give them more confidence, the rest of us went back into the boats. When he reached them, they made a great circle around him, touching him and gazing at him in wonderment, and while he was thus surrounded, we saw a woman come down the hill, and she carried a great club in her hand. When she reached to where our Christian stood encircled, she came behind him, and, lifting the club, gave him such a tremendous blow that she stretched him dead on the ground; in an instant the other women took hold of him by the feet and dragged him along towards the hill, and the men bounded towards the beach, and began to shoot at us with their bows and arrows. They put our people into such terror, with the boats being held fast by the small anchors that were sunk in the ground, that, because of the numerous arrows shot into the boats, no one thought to snatch up his arms. Finally, we fired four shots from the bombard at them, and immediately on hearing the explosions, they all fled towards the hill and to where the women were already cutting the Christian into bits, and at a great fire which they had made, were roasting him before our eyes, holding up several pieces towards us and then eating them: and the men made signs to us how they had killed the other two Christians and eaten them, which grieved us greatly.

What shocked us so much was seeing with our eyes the cruelty with which they treated the dead, which was an intolerable insult to all of us. We arranged that more than forty of us should land and avenge such cruel murder, and so bestial and inhuman an act, but the Admiral would not give his consent. We departed from them unwillingly, and with much shame, because of the decision of our captain.

WE LEFT THIS PLACE, and commenced our navigation by shaping a course between east and south. Thus we sailed along the land, making many landings, seeing natives, but having no dialogue with them. We sailed on until we found that the coast made a turn to the west when we had doubled a cape, to which we gave the name of the Cape of St Augustine. We then began to shape a course to the south-west. The cape is distant from the place where the Christians were murdered 150 leagues towards the east, and 8° from the equinoctial line to the south.

One day, we saw a great multitude of people on the beach, gazing at the wonderful sight of our ships. We turned the ship towards them, anchored in a good place, and went on shore with the boats. We found the people to be better conditioned than those we had met with before, and, responding to our overtures, they soon made friends, and traded with us. We were five days in this place, and found *canna fistola* very thick and green, and dry on the tops of the trees. We determined to take a pair of men from this place, that they might teach us their language, and three of them came voluntarily to go to Portugal.

Lest your Magnificence should be tired of so much writing, you must know that, on leaving this port, we sailed along on a westerly course, always in sight of land, continually making many landings, and speaking with an infinite number of people. We were so far south that we were outside the Tropic of Capricorn, where the South Pole rises above the horizon 32 degrees. We had lost sight altogether of Ursa Minor and Ursa Major, which were far below and scarcely seen on the horizon. We guided ourselves by the stars of the South Pole, which are numerous and much larger and brighter than those of our Pole. I traced the figure of the greater part of those of the first magnitude, with a declaration of their orbits round the South Pole, and of their diameters and semi-diameters. We sailed along that coast for 750 leagues, 150 from the cape called St Augustine, to the west, and 600 to the south.

Desiring to recount the things I saw on that coast, and what happened to us, as many more pages would not suffice me. On the coast we saw an infinite number of trees, brazil wood and cassia, and those trees which yield myrrh, as well as other marvels of nature which I am unable to recount. Having now been ten months on the voyage, and having seen that there was no mining wealth whatever in that land, we decided upon taking leave of it, and sailing across the sea for some other part. Having held a consultation, it was decided that the course should be taken which seemed good to me; and the command of the fleet was entrusted to me. I gave orders that the fleet should be supplied with wood and water for six months, such being the decision of the officers of the ships. Having made our departure from this land, we began our navigation with a southerly course on the 15th of February, when already the sun moved towards the equinoctial, and turned towards our Hemisphere of the North. We sailed so far on this course that we found ourselves where the South Pole had a height above our horizon of 52 degrees and we could no longer see the stars of Ursa Minor or of Ursa Major. We were then 500 leagues to the south of the port whence we had departed, and this was on the 3rd of April. On this day such a tempest arose on the sea that all our sails were blown away, and we ran under bare poles, with a heavy southerly gale and a tremendous sea, the air being very tempestuous. The gale was such that all the people in the fleet were much alarmed. The nights were very long - the one on the 7th of April lasted fifteen hours, the sun being at the end of Aries, and in that region it was winter, as your Magnificence will be well aware. Sailing in this storm, on the 7th of April we came in sight of new land, along which we ran for nearly 20 leagues, and found it all a rocky coast, without any port or inhabitants. [Probably South Georgia, or Tristan d'Acunha.] I believe this was because the cold was so great that no one in the fleet could endure it.

FINDING OURSELVES IN SUCH PERIL, and in such a storm that we could scarcely see one ship from another, owing to the greatness of the waves and the blinding mist, it was agreed with the principal captain that a signal should be made to the ships that they should make for land, and then shape a course for Portugal. This was very good counsel, for it is certain that if we had delayed another night all would have been lost; for, as we wore round the next day, we were met by such a storm that we expected to be swamped. We had to undertake pilgrimages and perform other ceremonies, as is the custom of sailors at such times. We ran for five days, always coming towards the equinoctial line, where the air and sea became more temperate. It pleased God to deliver us from such peril. Our course was now between the north and north-east, for our intention was to reach the coast of Ethiopia, our distance from it being 300 leagues, in the Gulf of the Atlantic Sea. By the grace of God, on the 10th day of May, we came in sight of land, where we were able to refresh ourselves, the land being called La Serra Liona. We were there fifteen days, and thence shaped a course to the islands of the Azores, which are distant nearly 750 leagues from that Sierra. We reached the islands in the end of July, where we remained fifteen days taking some recreation. Thence we departed for Lisbon, distant 300 leagues to the west, and arrived at that port of Lisbon on the 7th of September 1502, may God be thanked for our salvation, with only two ships. We burnt the other at Serra Liona, because she was no longer seaworthy. We were employed on this voyage nearly fifteen months; and for eleven days we navigated without seeing the North Star, nor the Great or Little Bears, which they call *el corno*, and we were guided by the stars of the other Pole. This is what I saw on this Voyage.

6

ALEXANDRINE TINNE - SEARCHING FOR
THE SOURCE OF THE NILE, 1853

*lexandrine Petronella Francina Tinne (1835-1869) was
a extremely wealthy Dutch woman of great personal
charm, with a zeal for adventure, and a spirit which
rebelled against the conventions of her age. In her mid-20s, she
made two expeditions in search of the source of the Nile and later
became the first European woman to attempt to cross the Sahara.*

*Alexine, as she liked to be called, was the daughter of a rich
Dutch merchant who settled in England during the Napoleonic
wars and later returned home. Her mother was Henriette van
Capellen, the daughter of a famous Dutch Vice-Admiral. Her
father died when she was 10 years old, leaving a fortune that
made her the richest woman in the Netherlands.*

*Inspired by stories of powerful women like Zenobia, the third-
century warrior queen of the Palmyrene Empire whose conquests
brought Egypt and most of the Roman East under her control,
Tinne moved to Damascus and visited the ruins of Palmyra.*

*In 1862, accompanied by her mother and aunt, she made her
first attempt to find the source of the Nile, but she fell ill and was
forced to return to Khartoum. They joined forces with two other
explorers, Theodor von Heuglin and Hermann Steudner, and*

decided to travel together to the Bahr-el-Ghazal, a tributary of the White Nile. It was a journey beset by difficulties, danger and death. Struck down by fever, both Steudner and Tinne's mother died; Tinne was once again forced to turn back to Khartoum, taking her mother's body with her.

The geographical and scientific results of the expedition were highly important, and news of it was first presented to the Royal Geographical Society in London in 1863, by Tinne's half-brother John. The men of the Society (no women were yet allowed to be members) expressed considerable surprise that "ladies" should be undertaking such a hazardous trip.

Undeterred by the setbacks and ignoring the pleas of relatives to return to Europe, Tinne was determined to try to cross the Sahara. She eventually set out from Tripoli in early 1968, aged 33. Early one morning, travelling between Murzuk and Ghat, her convoy was attacked by Tuareg warriors, and she and two Dutch sailors were stabbed to death. Her body was never recovered.

The account of the Nile expedition that we publish here are from letters sent to her half-brother, John Tinne, written by her mother. They formed the basis of his report to the Royal Geographical Society.

'THE MERCHANTS BUY IVORY, BECOME MASTERS, AND ATTACK NEIGHBOURING VILLAGES; HAVING GUNS, OF COURSE, THEY SUCCEED'

MISHRA OF EEK, 26th March, 1863.

I write at present from one of the most singular spots on the globe, which can only be reached by a route as singular. We pushed along up the Ghazal for three or four days, the river in front always appearing to have come to an end in a sea of herbage, alternating with bulrushes, etc. It proves, however, to be an immense marsh, through which the boats are slowly pushed, the brushwood being beaten down with sticks, or cut with hatchets and scythes.

After four days of this exhausting work we arrived at a small pond or lagoon, in which were crowded together, in the utmost confusion, twenty-five vessels of various descriptions. This was the Mishra or port of Eek. Here we had to stay to get porters, and only now can detail our plans. Dr Heuglin has gone eight or ten days inland, to see whether he can find any, when we shall proceed to the spot selected for our passing the rainy season. The equipment of the expedition is something incredible, as we must carry with us ten months' provisions and stores - amongst other things, a ton and a half of beads, 8 bars of copper, 12,000 cowrie shells, pepper, salt, etc.; and as each porter only carries 40 lbs load, you can form an idea of the immense number we shall require - above 200 porters at the very least.

There is absolutely no traffic along the river, except for the naggars or merchandise boats in search of ivory; a pair of tusks fetching at Khartoum perhaps £25. These naggars convey provisions to the various stations or *zeribas*, as they are called, taking back ivory in exchange.

May 13. All is well now; we have 80 porters; we know whither we are bound; in short, all is right. Dr Heuglin is quite pleased with the interior - pretty country, good water, and hospitable people, and is enchanted with the birds; quite rare and new, he says.

We have had a visit from Mr and Mrs Petherick [The British consul in Karthoum and his wife], who, hearing we were here at the Mishra, came to see us to offer to be of use to us, which they have been in many respects. They have had dreadful ill luck. They set off too late from Khartoum in March, and the wind being adverse caused them much delay and damage, so they had to abandon their boats and proceed by land from Abukaka. This was the end of August, 1862; and it being the rainy season, that plan proved equally impracticable. They were delayed by affrays with inhospitable natives and by illness, and only arrived at Gondokoro in February last, five days after Captain Speke, who, not knowing what had become of them, and believing them from the current reports to be drowned, accepted Mr Baker's provisions, boat, and men, so that the Pethericks had to retain all they had sent forward for Captain Speke's requirements. These we have taken over from them - beer, wine, tea, soup, pearl barley, Leman's biscuits, a gutta percha boat, and what not. It is strange to find these luxuries here, and we have enjoyed them famously.

JUNE 1. We left our boats on the 17th May, and landed our baggage, in order that the porters might see what they had to carry. I cannot say that the first part of the country is pretty, but it is very peculiar; the trees beautiful, with a succession of neat villages, and pools of water. We arrived at a village called Afog on the 20th. Here my daughter fell ill with fever; and the next day our soldiers rebelled. They complained that they had nothing to eat, although they had five bullocks a day; then they said they had not enough doura (grain of the country); but after some patient remonstrances, they all came, one by one, to beg pardon. So we arranged that as many as we could spare should go on to Ali-au-Mori's station.

Once more en route, we shall, I trust, arrive safe and sound at the mountain, Casinka, where we are to remain till the weather is fine and the earth dry. It must be a beautiful country, plenty of game, and very good people, though no Europeans have been there. We have already sent off three companies of porters, about 400 men in all. They carry but little, say 40 lbs each, and all on their heads.

Afog, where we are staying, is a very pretty village, with rich cultivated patches, full of doura, besides a sort of ground-nuts and quantities of pumpkins. The trees are magnificent, and the cows, goats, and sheep abundant. The people live in beehive-looking huts, of which each family has three or four, for themselves and flocks. We have rivers to pass before we come to where we hope to stay, near the mountain Casinka. And we are now going to Ali-au-Mori's *zeriba*, where we have sent on all our provisions. From there we hope to cross to Casinka ; and thence we are only two days from the Nyam-Nyam, our goal.

JULY 1. I know you will be glad to hear how, after all our trouble and expense, the new country pleases us, and that, though still weak and subject to attacks of fever, our invalids stand the journey very well: my daughter has a *ngerib*, arranged with a covering to keep off the sun, and her mattress on it, so that she reposes very agreeably. We have 192 negroes for our immediate luggage; we have 38 donkeys, but they suffer so much from climate and neglect, and are so cruelly overburdened when we allow them to be loaded at all, that now they are kept for the sick or tired human beings. We take very short journeys, and always find a village to sleep in. The two first days, after leaving the Mishra, was not pretty; but there were some beautiful trees and so many rich villages, that it could not be called ugly; thousands of birds made it gay - such beautiful stations, belonging to rich negroes or merchants, such neat houses, surrounded by a high hedge of the poison-plant, and such a number of cows and sheep. After a while the trees became thicker and higher, and we were one whole day's journey in a wood of gardenias in full bloom, with jasmine and sensitive-plants. Afterwards the woods became forests of high majestic trees, and the ground covered with sweetest flowers; we had not time to pick many, as we are hurrying on. We crossed the river Djour on the 16th June, which took only six minutes for each party: but there were only seven boats for all our luggage and people.

You can form no idea of the frequency and intensity of the storms - wind, hail, rain, thunder, and lightning - which makes us all the more anxious to reach our camping-ground for the rainy season. We had one on our landing from our boats at the Mishra; another just after our arrival at Afog, while we were pitching our tents; that of my daughter was blown down when half up, and herself nearly smothered in its folds. The severe cold and wetting she then experienced brought on a fever, which prostrated her for more than a week, and, as already mentioned, brought her almost to death's door. Our last experience was just after crossing the Djour, when, not having succeeded, owing to the stupidity of the *vakeel* [agent, or representative], in bringing over our tents and baggage, the whole party were exposed throughout the night to the pelting of the storm, there being no village or shelter of any sort near. Fortunately the storm had no evil effect upon the health of any one of the party.

I am writing this in the village where poor Dr Steudner died. We did not meet a caravan, as we expected, and came on 21st June to a *zeriba* or village belonging to Buselli, a foreign merchant of Khartoum, whose reception of us was magnificent, but who proved afterwards most extortionate.

We are going to hire a small *zeriba* he has for 30 thalers, which we succeeded in getting, after he had attempted suddenly to charge 200 thalers. But it is impossible to tell how he teased us. First he turned out all our soldiers, and when we built a shed for them he asked hire for it! Then he has once offered and refused negroes, and changes his terms every day; one day lets us have as much doura as we want, another refuses to let us have anything for our people to eat, and tries to make us pay 9 thalers for what costs at Khartoum only one. The whole country is one field of doura, yet he will not permit his negroes to sell us any.

The origin and system of these merchants are different here from the White Nile. A man comes into a village, sets himself down, and begins by buying ivory and making friends with the negroes, promises to protect them if they will take the ivory to the ships in the Mishra, and he either remains himself or leaves a *vakeel*. He builds a house or two, surrounds it with palisades, and, by degrees becoming master of the village, then proceeds to attack a neighbouring hostile village, and, having guns, of course they conquer. That village he attaches to the first, and so on till he has a good many villages, when he forces the negroes of the whole to furnish doura for his soldiers or fighting men, and they submit.

We heard today from a party coming down from Casinka that it is no longer possible to reach the mountain before the rains: we shall, therefore, be shut up for the next four months, but it is very safe. There is no chance of our being able to come back here to rejoin our boats till December or January next. The rains do not finish till November, and then the rivers are so swollen, and the mud so deep, no animals can pass, nor are there any boats for us - nothing but a hollowed-out tree or a bundle of sticks joined together, which the blacks go about on: however, we shall make it out as well as we can.

There is abundance of game everywhere. Of quadrupeds, we have seen giraffes and gazelles, and the recent tracks of elephants and buffaloes, large herds of which Dr Heuglin fell in with on his previous short visit, when in search of porters, but they are now scared away by the noise of our large caravan. Of birds, there are francolin (rails), black partridges, and guinea fowls. Dr Heuglin has collected specimens of 60 new and rare sorts of birds, which he has sent to the Museum of the University of Leyden.

7

IBN BATTUTA - THE MERCURIAL SULTAN
OF DELHI, 1334-42

*bu Abdullah Muhammad Ibn Battuta (1304-c.1368) is
regarded as the greatest traveller of premodern times,
a man who paved the way for the modern age of
discovery. Born in Tangier, Morocco, he first left his homeland at
the age of 21 to make the holy pilgrimage to Mecca. It was the
start of an extraordinary life of travel that covered almost 30
years, some 73,000 miles (117,000km), and took in the Middle
East, present-day West and North Africa, Pakistan, Afghanistan,
India, The Maldives, Sri Lanka and China.*

He left behind a long written account of his travels, Rihla,
*that has given historians a unique glimpse into the medieval
world, its peoples and its customs.*

*Battuta somehow survived some close shaves during his
odyssey. While travelling from Alexandria to the Maghreb, he
twice narrowly escaped being captured by European pirates. He
was harassed by Hindu rebels on his journey from India to
China, and he was later kidnapped and robbed of everything but
his trousers and his prayer mat. When he eventually reached
safety, some ships that he was about to board were blown out to*

sea in a storm and sank, killing many in his party. Throughout, Battuta's Islamic faith remained steadfast; at one stage, he adopted an ascetic life, resigning all his posts and giving away all his possessions.

The edited excerpt published here concerns his time in India. Arriving in Delhi in 1334, he gained employment as a judge under Muhammad Tughluq, a powerful and mercurial Islamic sultan. Battuta passed several years here but he gradually grew wary of his employer, who was known to maim and kill his enemies and those who caused him displeasure - sometimes by tossing them to elephants with swords attached to their tusks. He was finally able to escape the sultan's clutches when, in 1341, he was selected to be his envoy to the Mongol court of China.

'THE MASTER OF THE WORLD'S PALACE IS NEVER WITHOUT SOME POOR MAN ENRICHED, OR SOME LIVING MAN EXECUTED'

THE FIRST TOWN we reached after leaving Multin was Abohar, which is the first town in India proper, and thence we entered a plain extending for a day's journey. On the borders of this plain are inaccessible mountains, inhabited by Hindu infidels; some of them are subjects under Muslim rule, and live in villages governed by a Muslim headman appointed by the governor in whose fief the village lies. Others of them are rebels and warriors, who maintain themselves in the fatnesses of the mountains and make plundering raids.

On this road we fell in with a raiding party, this being the first engagement I witnessed in India. The main party had left Abohar in the early morning, but I had stayed there with a small party of my companions until midday and when we left, numbering in all twenty-two horsemen, partly Arabs and partly Persians and Turks, we were attacked on this plain by eighty infidels on foot with two horsemen. My companions were men of courage and ability and we fought stoutly with them, killing one of the horsemen and about twelve of the footsoldiers. I was hit by an arrow and my horse by another, but God preserved me from them, for there is no force in their arrows. One of our party had his horse wounded, but we gave him in exchange the horse we had captured from the infidel, and killed the wounded horse, which was eaten by the Turks of our party. We carried the heads of the slain to the castle of Abii Bak'har, which we reached about midnight, and suspended them from the wall.

Two days later, we reached Ajiidahan [now Pakpattan, Pakistan], a small town belonging to the pious Shaykh Farid ad-Din. As I returned to the camp after visiting him, I saw the people hurrying out, and some of our party along with them. I asked them what was happening and they told me that one of the Hindu infidels had died, that a fire had been kindled to burn him, and his wife would burn herself along with him. After the burning, my companions came back and told me that she had embraced the dead man until she herself was burned with him. Later on I used often to see a Hindu woman, richly dressed, riding on horseback, followed by both Muslims and infidels and preceded by drums and trumpets; she was accompanied by Brahmins, who are the chiefs of the Hindus. In the sultan's dominions, they ask his permission to burn her, which he accords them. The burning of the wife after her husband's death is regarded by them as a commendable act, but is not compulsory; only when a widow burns herself her family acquire a certain prestige by it and gain a reputation for fidelity. A widow who does not burn herself dresses in coarse garments and lives with her own people in misery, despised for her lack of fidelity, but she is not forced to burn herself. Once in the town of Amjhera, I saw three women whose husbands had been killed in battle and who had agreed to burn themselves. Each one had a horse brought to her and mounted it, richly dressed and perfumed. In her right hand she held a coconut, with which she played, and in her left a mirror, in which she looked at her face. They were surrounded by Brahmins and their own relatives, and were preceded by drums, trumpets and bugles. Everyone of the infidels said to them "Take greetings from me to my father, or brother or mother, or friend " and they would say "Yes" and smile at them. I rode out with my companions to see the way in which the burning was carried out.

AFTER THREE MILES we came to a dark place with much water and shady trees, amongst which there were four pavilions, each containing a stone idol. Between the pavilions there was a basin of water over which a dense shade was cast by trees so thickly set that the sun could not penetrate them. The place looked like a spot in hell - God preserve us from it! On reaching these pavilions they descended to the pool, plunged into it and diverted themselves of their clothes and ornaments, which they distributed as alms. Each one was then given an unsewn garment of coarse cotton and tied part of it round her waist and part over her head and shoulders. The fires had been lit near this basin in a low lying spot, and oil of sesame poured over them, so that the flames were increased. There were about fifteen men there with faggots of thin wood and about ten others with heavy pieces of wood, and the drummers and trumpeters were standing by waiting for the woman's coming. The fire was screened off by a blanket held by some men, so that she should not be frightened by the sight of it. I saw one woman, on coming to the blanket, pull it violently out of the men's hands, saying to them with a smile: "Do you frighten me with the fire? I know that it is a fire, so let me alone."

Thereupon she joined her hands above her head in salutation to the fire and cast herself into it. At the same moment, the drums, trumpets and bugles were sounded, the men threw their firewood on her and the others put the heavy wood on top of her to prevent her moving, cries were raised and there was a loud clamour. When I saw this I had all but fallen off my horse, if my companions had not quickly brought water to me and washed my face, after which I withdrew.

The Indians have a similar practice of drowning themselves and many of them do so in the river Ganges, the river to which they go on pilgrimage, and into which the ashes of those who are burned are cast. They say that it is a river of Paradise. When one of them comes to drown himself he says to those present with him, "Do not think that I drown myself for any worldly reason or through penury; my purpose is solely to seek approach to Kusay." Kusay being the name of God in their language. He then drowns himself, and when he is dead they take him out and burn him and cast his ashes into this river.

LET us return to our original topic. We set out from the town of Ajiidahan, and after four days march reached Sarasati, a large town with quantities of rice of an excellent sort which is exported to the capital, Delhi. The town produces a large revenue; I was told how much it is, but have forgotten the figure. Thence we travelled to Hansi, an exceedingly fine, well built and populous city, surrounded by a wall. Two days later, we came to Mas'dd Abad, which is ten miles from Delhi, and there we spent three days. The sultan was away at the time in the district of the town of Qanawj, which is ten days' march from Delhi, but the queen-mother was in the capital, and the sultan's *wazir*. He sent his officers to receive us, designating for each one of us a person of his own rank. Meanwhile, he wrote to inform the sultan of our arrival, sending the letter by courier post, and received the sultan's reply during the three days that we spent at Mas'dd Abad. Thereafter the qidis, doctors and shaykhs, and some of the amirs came out to meet us. The Indians call the amirs "kings", using the term "king" where the people of Diyar-Bakr, Egypt, and elsewhere say "amir". We then set out from Mas'dd Abad and halted near a village called Palam. On the next day we arrived at the city of Delhi, the metropolis of India, a vast and magnificent city, uniting beauty with strength. It is surrounded by a wall that has no equal in the world, and is the largest city in India, nay rather the largest city in the entire Muslim Orient.

The city of Delhi is made up now of four neighbouring and contiguous towns. One of them is Delhi proper, the old city built by the infidels and captured in the year 1188. The second is called Siri, known also as the Abode of the Caliphate; this was the town given by the sultan to Ghiydth ad-Din, the grandson of the Abbasid Caliph Muftansir, when he came to his court. The third is called Tughlaq Abad, after its founder, the Sultan Tughlaq, the father of the sultan of India to whose court we came.

The reason why he built it was that one day, he said to a former sultan: "Oh Master of the World, it is fitting that a city should be built here." The sultan replied to him in jest, "When you are sultan, build it." It came about by the decree of God that he became sultan, so he built it and called it by his own name. The fourth is called Jahan Pandh, and is set apart for the residence of the reigning sultan, Muhammad Shah. He was the founder of it, and it was his intention to unite these four towns within a single wall, but after building part of it he gave up the rest because of the expense required for its construction.

The cathedral mosque occupies a large area; its walls, roof, and paving are all constructed of white stones, admirably squared and firmly cemented with lead. There is no wood in it at all. It has thirteen domes of stone, its pulpit also is made of stone, and it has four courts. In the centre of the mosque is an awe-inspiring column, and nobody knows of what metal it is constructed. One of their learned men told me that it is called Haft Jish, which means "seven metals", and that it is constructed from these seven. A part of this column, of a finger's breadth, has been polished, and gives out a brilliant gleam. Iron makes no impression on it. It is thirty cubits high, and we rolled a turban round it, and the portion which encircled it measured eight cubits. At the eastern gate there are two enormous idols of brass prostrate on the ground and held by stones, and everyone entering or leaving the mosque treads on them. The site was formerly occupied by an idol temple, and was converted into a mosque on the conquest of the city. In the northern court is the minaret, which has no parallel in the lands of Islam. It is built of red stone, unlike the rest of the edifice, ornamented with sculptures, and of great height. The ball on the top is of glistening white marble and its "apples" [small balls] are of pure gold. The passage is so wide that elephants could go up by it.

A person in whom I have confidence told me that when it was built he saw an elephant climbing with stones to the top. The Sultan Qutb ad-Din wished to build one in the western court even larger, but was cut off by death when only a third of it had been completed. This minaret is one of the wonders of the world for size, and the width of its passage is such that three elephants could mount it abreast. The third of it built equals in height the whole of the other minaret we have mentioned in the northern court, though to one looking at it from below it does not seem so high because of its bulk.

Outside Delhi is a large reservoir named after the Sultan Lalmish, from which the inhabitants draw their drinking water. It is supplied by rain water, and is about two miles in length by half that breadth. In the centre there is a great pavilion built of squared stones, two storeys high. When the reservoir is filled with water it can be reached only in boats, but when the water is low the people go into it. Inside it is a mosque, and at most times it is occupied by mendicants devoted to the service of God. When the water dries up at the sides of this reservoir, they sow sugar canes, cucumbers, green melons and pumpkins there. The melons and pumpkins are very sweet but of small size. Between Delhi and the Abode of the Caliphate is the private reservoir, which is larger than the other. Along its sides there are about forty pavilions, and round about it live the musicians.

Among the learned and pious inhabitants of Delhi is the devout and humble imam Kamil ad-Din, called "The Cave Man" from the cave in which he lives outside the city. I had a slave-boy who ran away from me, and whom I found in the possession of a certain Turk. I proposed to take him back from him, but the sheikh said to me, "This boy is no good to you. Don't take him." The Turk wished to come to an arrangement, so he paid me a hundred dinars and kept the boy. Six months later the boy killed his master and was taken before the sultan, who ordered him to be handed over to his master's sons, and they put him to death. When I saw this miracle on the part of the sheikh, I attached myself to him, withdrawing from the world and giving all that I possessed to the poor and needy. I stayed with him for some time, and I used to see him fast for ten and twenty days on end and remain standing most of the night. I continued with him until the sultan sent for me and I became entangled in the world once again - may God give me a good ending!

THIS KING IS of all men the fondest of making gifts and of shedding blood. His gate is never without some poor man enriched or some living man executed, and stories are current amongst the people of his generosity and courage and of his cruelty and violence towards criminals. For all that, he is of all men the most humble and the readiest to show equity and justice. The ceremonies of religion are swiftly complied with at his court, and he is severe in the matter of attendance at prayer and in punishing those who neglect it. He is one of those kings whose felicity is unimpaired and surpassing all ordinary experience, but his dominant quality is generosity.

We shall relate some stories of this that are marvellous beyond anything ever heard before, and I call God and his Angels and His Prophets to witness that all that I tell of his extraordinary generosity is absolute truth. I know that some of the instances I shall relate will be unacceptable to the minds of many, and that they will regard them as quite impossible, but in a matter which I have seen with my own eyes and of which I know the accuracy and have had a large share, I cannot do otherwise than speak the truth.

The sultan's palace at Delhi is called Dar Sara, and contains many doors. At the first door there are a number of guardians, and beside it trumpeters and flute-players. When any amir or person of note arrives, they sound their instruments and say, "So-and-so has come, so-and-so has come." The same takes place also at the second and third doors. Outside the first door are platforms on which the executioners sit, for the custom amongst them is that when the sultan orders a man to be executed, the sentence is carried out at the door of the audience hall, and the body lies there over three nights. Between the first and second doors there is a large vestibule with platforms along both sides, on which sit those whose turn of duty it is to guard the doors.

Between the second and third doors there is a large platform on which the principal *naqib* [keeper of the register] sits; in front of him there is a gold mace, which he holds in his hand, and on his head he wears a jewelled tiara of gold, surmounted by peacock feathers. The second door leads to an extensive audience hall in which the people sit. At the third door there are platforms occupied by the scribes of the door. One of their customs is that none may pass through this door except those whom the sultan has prescribed, and for each person he prescribes a number of his staff to enter along with him. Whenever any person comes to this door the scribes write down "So-and-so came at the first hour" or the second, and so on, and the sultan receives a report of this after the evening prayer. Another of their customs is that anyone who absents himself from the palace for three days or more, with or without excuse, may not enter this door thereafter except by the sultan's permission. If he has an excuse of illness or otherwise, he presents the sultan with a gift suitable to his rank. The third door opens into an immense audience hall called Hazar Ustun, which means "a thousand pillars". The pillars are of wood and support a wooden roof, admirably carved. The people sit under this, and it is in this hall that the sultan holds public audiences.

As a rule, his audiences are held in the afternoon, though he often holds them early in the day. He sits cross-legged on a throne placed on a dais carpeted in white, with a large cushion behind him and two others as arm-rests on his right and left. When he takes his seat, the *wazir* stands in front of him, the secretaries behind the *wazir*, then the chamberlains and so on in order of precedence.

As the sultan sits down the chamberlains and *naqibs* say in their loudest voice "*Bismillah*" [*which translates as "In the name of God"*]. At the sultan's head stands the "great king" Qabiila with a fly-whisk in his hand to drive off the flies. A hundred armour-bearers stand on the right and a like number on the left, carrying shields, swords, and bows. The other functionaries and notables stand along the hall to right and left. Then they bring in sixty horses with the royal harness, half of which are ranged on the right and half on the left, where the sultan can see them. Next fifty elephants are brought in, which are adorned with silken cloths, and have their tusks shod with iron for greater efficacy in killing criminals. On the neck of each elephant is its *mahout*, who carries a sort of iron axe with which he punishes it and directs it to do what is required of it. Each elephant has on its back a sort of large chest capable of holding twenty warriors or more or less, according to the size of the beast. These elephants are trained to make obeisance to the sultan and incline their heads, and when they do so the chamberlains cry in a loud voice "*Bismillah*". They also are arranged half on the right and half on the left behind the persons standing. As each person enters who has an appointed place of standing on the right or left, he makes obeisance on reaching the station of the chamberlains, and the chamberlains say *"Bismillah"*, regulating the loudness of their utterance by the rank of the person concerned, who then retires to his appointed place, beyond which he never passes. If it is one of the infidel Hindus who makes obeisance, the chamberlains say to him, "God guide thee."

If there should be anyone at the door who has come to offer the sultan a gift, the chamberlains enter the sultan's presence in order of precedence, make obeisance in three places, and inform the sultan of the person at the door. If he commands them to bring him in, they place the gift in the hands of men who stand with it in front of the sultan where he can see it. He then calls in the donor, who makes obeisance three times before reaching the sultan and makes another obeisance at the station of the chamberlains. The sultan then addresses him in person with the greatest courtesy and bids him welcome. If he is a person who is worthy of honour, the sultan takes him by the hand or embraces him, and asks for some part of his present. It is then placed before him, and if it consists of weapons or fabrics he turns it this way and that with his hand and expresses his approval, to set the donor at ease and encourage him. He gives him a robe of honour and assigns him a sum of money to wash his head, according to their custom in this case, proportioned to his merits.

When the sultan returns from a journey, the elephants are decorated, and on sixteen of them are placed sixteen parasols, some brocaded and some set with jewels. Wooden pavilions are built several storeys high and covered with silk cloths, and in each storey there are singing girls wearing magnificent dresses and ornaments, with dancing girls amongst them. In the centre of each pavilion is a large tank made of skins and filled with syrup-water, from which all the people, natives or strangers, may drink, receiving at the same time betel leaves and areca nuts. The space between the pavilions is carpeted with silk cloths, on which the sultan's horse treads. The walls of the street along which he passes from the gate of the city to the gate of the palace are hung with silk cloths. In front of him march footmen from his own slaves, several thousands in number, and behind come the mob and the soldiers. On one of his entries into the capital, I saw three or four small catapults placed on elephants throwing gold and silver coins amongst the people from the moment when he entered the city until he reached the palace.

I SHALL NOW MENTION a few of his magnificent gifts and largesses. The merchant Shihab ad-Din of Kazarun, who was a friend of al-Kazarfini, the "king" of the merchants in India, was invited by the latter to join him and arrived with a valuable present for the sultan. On their way, they were attacked by a considerable force of infidels, who killed the "king" of the merchants and carried off as booty his money and treasures and Shihab ad-Din's present. Shihab ad-Din himself escaped with his life, and the sultan, on hearing of this, gave orders that he should be given thirty thousand dinars and return to his own country. He refused to accept it, however, saying that he had come for the express purpose of seeing the sultan and kissing the ground before him. They wrote to the sultan to this effect and he, gratified with what Shihab ad-Din had said, commanded him to be brought to Delhi with every mark of honour.

When Shihab ad-Din was introduced into the sultan's presence, the sultan made him a rich present, and some days later asked where he was. On hearing that he was ill, he commanded one of his courtiers to go instantly to the treasury and take a hundred thousand tangahs of gold (the tangah being worth two and a half Moroccan dinars) and carry them to him to set him at ease. He ordered him to buy with this money what Indian goods he pleased, and gave instructions that no one else should buy anything at all until Shihab ad-Din had made all his purchases. In addition, he ordered three ships to be made ready for his journey with complete equipment and full pay and provisions for the crew. So Shihab ad-Din departed and disembarked in the island of Hormuz, where he built a great house. I saw this house later on, and I saw also Shihab ad-Din, having lost all that he had, soliciting a gift at Shiraz from its sultan, Abu Ishaq. That is the way with riches amassed in these Indian lands; it is only rarely that anyone gets out of the country with them, and when he does leave it and reaches some other country, God sends upon him some calamity which annihilates all that he possesses. So it happened to Shihab ad-Din, for everything that he had was taken from him in the civil war between the king of Hormuz and his nephews, and he left the country stripped of all his wealth.

The doctor Shams ad-Din, who was a philosopher and a born poet, wrote a laudatory ode to the sultan in Persian. The ode contained twenty-seven verses, and the sultan gave him a thousand silver dinars for each verse. This is more than has ever been related of former kings, for they used to give a thousand dirhams for each verse, which is only a tenth of the sultan's gift. Then, too, when the sultan heard the story of the learned and pious *qadi* Majd ad-Din of Shiraz, he sent ten thousand silver dinars to him at Shiraz.

Again, Burhdn ad-Din was a preacher and imam so liberal in spending what he possessed that he used often to run up debts in order to give to others. The sultan heard of him and sent him forty thousand dinars, with a request that he would come to Delhi. He accepted the gift and paid his debts with it, but went off to Cathay and refused to come to the sultan, saying "I shall not go to a sultan in whose presence scholars have to stand."

One of the Indian nobles claimed that the sultan had put his brother to death without cause, and cited him before the *qadi*. The sultan walked on foot and unarmed to the *qadi's* tribunal, saluted him and made obeisance, having previously commanded the *qadi* not to rise before him or move when he entered his court, and remained standing before him. The *qadi* gave judgment against the sultan, to the effect that he must give satisfaction to his adversary for the blood of his brother, and he did so. At another time, a certain Muslim claimed that the sultan owed him a sum of money. They carried the matter before the *qadi*, who gave judgment against the sultan for the payment of the debt, and he paid it.

When a famine broke out in India and Sind, and prices became so high that a maund of wheat rose to six dinars, the sultan ordered that every person in Delhi should be given six months' provisions from the granary, at the rate of a pound and a half per person per day, small or great, freeman or slave. The doctors and *qadis* set about compiling registers of the population of each quarter and brought the people, each of whom received six months' provisions.

IN SPITE of all we have said of his humility, justice, compassion for the needy, and extraordinary generosity, the sultan was far too ready to shed blood. He punished small faults and great, without respect of persons, whether men of learning, piety, or high station. Every day hundreds of people, chained, pinioned, and fettered, are brought to his hall, and those who are for execution are executed, those for torture tortured, and those for beating beaten. It is his custom that every day all persons who are in his prison are brought to the hall, except only on Fridays; this is a day of respite for them, on which they clean themselves and remain at ease - may God deliver us from misfortune! The sultan had a half-brother named Masud Khan, whose mother was the daughter of Sultan Ala ad-Din, and who was one of the most beautiful men I have ever seen on earth. He suspected him of wishing to revolt, and questioned him on the matter. Masud confessed through fear of torture, for anyone who denies an accusation of this sort which the sultan formulates against him is put to the torture, and the people consider death a lighter affliction than torture. The sultan gave orders that he should be beheaded in the marketplace, and his body lay there for three days according to their custom.

One of the gravest charges against the sultan is that of compelling the inhabitants of Delhi to leave the town. The reason for this was that they used to write missives reviling and insulting him, seal them and inscribe them, "By the hand of the Master of the World, none but he may read this." They then threw them into the audience-hall at night, and when the sultan broke the seal he found them full of insults and abuse. He decided to lay Delhi in ruins, and having bought from all the inhabitants their houses and dwellings and paid them the price of them, he commanded them to move to Dawlat Abad. They refused, and his herald was sent to proclaim that no person should remain in the city after three nights. The majority complied with the order, but some of them hid in the houses. The sultan ordered a search to be made for any persons remaining in the town, and his slaves found two men in the streets, one a cripple and the other blind. They were brought before him and he gave orders that the cripple should be flung from a mangonel [catapult] and the blind man dragged from Delhi to Dawlat Abad, a journey of forty days. He fell to pieces on the road and all that reached Dawlat Abad was his leg. When the sultan did this, every person left the town, abandoning furniture and possessions, and the city remained utterly deserted. A person in whom I have confidence told me that the sultan mounted one night to the roof of his palace and looked out over Delhi, where there was neither smoke nor lamp, and said, "Now my mind is tranquil and my wrath appeased." Afterwards he wrote to the inhabitants of the other cities commanding them to move to Delhi to repopulate it. The result was only to ruin their cities and leave Delhi still unpopulated, because of its immensity, for it is one of the greatest cities in the world. It was in this state that we found it on our arrival, empty and unpopulated, save for a few inhabitants.

LET us return now to that which concerns us, and relate how we arrived first at the capital and our fortunes until we left his service. We reached Delhi during the sultan's absence, and proceeded to the palace, where, after passing the first, second, and third doors, the principal *naqib* introduced us into a spacious audience hall. Here we found the *wazir* awaiting us.

On passing through the third door, the great hall called Hazar Ustin, where the sultan holds his public audiences, met our eyes. Thereupon the *wazir* made obeisance until his head nearly touched the ground, and we too made obeisance by inclining the body and touching the ground with our fingers, in the direction of the sultan's throne. When we had performed this ceremony, the *naqibs* cried in a loud voice "Bismillah", and we all retired.

After visiting the palace of the sultan's mother and presenting her with a gift, we returned to the house which had been prepared for our occupation, and hospitality-gifts were sent to us. In the house I found everything that was required in the way of furniture, carpets, mats, vessels, and bed. The beds in India are light, and can be carried by a single man; every person when travelling has to transport his own bed, which his slave boy carries on his head. It consists of four conical legs with four cross pieces of wood on which braids of silk or cotton are woven.

When one lies down on it, there is no need for anything to make it pliable, for it is pliable of itself. Along with the bed they brought two mattresses and pillows and a coverlet, all made of silk. Their custom is to put linen or cotton slips on the mattresses and coverlets, so that when they become dirty they wash the slips, while the bedding inside is kept clean. Next day we rode to the palace to salute the *wazir*, who gave me two purses, each containing a thousand silver dinars, saying "This is for washing your head", and in addition gave me a robe of fine goats hair.

A list was made of all my companions, servants, and slave boys, and they were divided into four categories; those in the first category each received two hundred dinars, in the second a hundred and fifty, the third a hundred, and the fourth sixty-five. There were about forty of them, and the total sum given to them was four thousand odd dinars. After that the sultan's hospitality gift was fixed. This was composed of a thousand pounds of Indian flour, a thousand pounds of flesh-meat, and I cannot say how many pounds of sugar, ghee, and areca nuts, with a thousand betel leaves. The Indian pound equals twenty of our Moroccan pounds and twenty-five Egyptian pounds. Later on, the sultan commanded some villages to be assigned to me to the yearly revenue of five thousand dinars.

On the 4th of Shawwal [8th June, 1334] the sultan returned to the castle of Tilbat, seven miles from the capital, and the *wazir* ordered us to go out to him. We set out, each man with his present of horses, camels, fruits, swords, etc., and assembled at the gate of the castle. The newcomers were introduced in order of precedence and were given robes of linen, embroidered in gold. When my turn came I entered and found the sultan seated on a chair. At first, I took him to be one of the chamberlains. When I had twice made obeisance the "king" of the Sultan's intimate courtiers said "*Bismillah*, Mawlana Badr ad-Din", for in India they used to call me Badr ad-Din, and Mawlana ["Our Master"] is a title given to all scholars.

I approached the sultan, who took my hand and shook it, and continuing to hold it addressed me most affably in Persian, saying: "Your arrival is blessed; be at ease, I shall be compassionate to you and give you such favours that your fellow-countrymen will hear of it and come to join you." Then he asked me where I came from and I answered him, and every time he said any encouraging word to me I kissed his hand, until I had kissed it seven times. All the new arrivals then assembled and a meal was served to them.

Afterwards, the sultan used to summon us to eat in his presence and would enquire how we fared and address us most affably. He assigned us pensions, giving me twelve thousand dinars a year, and added two villages to the three he had already commanded for me. One day he sent the *wazir* and the governor of Sind to us to say, "The Master of the World says, 'Whoever amongst you is capable of undertaking the function of *wazir* or secretary or commander or judge or professor or shaykh, I shall appoint to that office.'" Everyone was silent at first, for what they were wanting was to gain riches and return to their countries. After some of the others had spoken, the *wazir* said to me in Arabic, "What do you say?" I replied, "*Wazirships* and secretaryships are not my business, but as to *qadis* and sheikhs, that is my occupation, and the occupation of my fathers before me." The sultan was pleased with what I had said, and I was summoned to the palace to do homage on appointment as *qadi* of the Malikite rite at Delhi.

IT HAPPENS OFTEN that there is a long delay in the payment of the money gifts of the sultan (though they are always paid in the end) and I waited six months before receiving the twelve thousand dinars promised to me. They have a custom also of deducting a tenth from all sums given by the sultan. Now, as I have related, I had borrowed from the merchants for the expenses of my journey and my present to the sultan, as well as for my residence at Delhi. When they prepared to return to their country, they importuned me to pay my debts, so I wrote a long poem in praise of the sultan and presented it to him. He received it with pleasure, and I was congratulated by everyone. After waiting for some time, I wrote a petition and transmitted it to the sultan, who ordered the *wazir* to pay my debts. The *wazir* delayed for some days, and meanwhile received orders to proceed to Dawlat Abad. During this time the sultan had gone out hunting; the *wazir* set off, and I received nothing at all until some time later.

When my creditors were ready to travel, I said to them, "When I go to the palace, claim your debt from me according to the custom in this country", for I knew that when the sultan learned of that he would pay them. Their custom is this; the creditor awaits the debtor at the door of the palace, and when the debtor is on the point of entering he says to him, "Oh enemy of the sultan, by the head of the sultan you shall not enter until you have paid me." The debtor may not leave the place after that until he pays him or obtains a delay from him. They did this, and the sultan sent a chamberlain to ask the merchants the amount of the debt. They replied: "Fifty-five thousand dinars."

The sultan then sent the chamberlain to say to them, "The Master of the World says to you, 'The money is in my possession, and I shall give you justice; do not demand it of him.'" He then commanded two officers to sit in the Hall of the Thousand Columns to examine and verify the creditors' documents. They found them in order and informed the sultan, who laughed and said, "I know he is a *qadi* and has seen to his business with them." He then commanded the treasurer to pay the sum, but the treasurer greedily demanded a bribe for doing so and would not write the order. I sent him two hundred tangahs, but he returned them. One of his servants told me from him that he wanted five hundred tangahs and I refused to pay it. The matter came to the ears of the sultan, who in great displeasure ordered payment to be suspended until the treasurer's conduct was investigated.

Later on, when the sultan went out to hunt, I went out along with him at once, as I had already prepared all that is required according to the habits of the Indians, and had hired bearers, grooms, valets, and runners. One day, when the sultan was in his tent he enquired who were outside. Nasir ad-Din, one of his courtiers, said, "So-and-so, the Moroccan, who is very upset." "Why so?" asked the sultan, and he replied, "Because of his debt, since his creditors are pressing for payment. The Master of the World had commanded the *wazir* to pay it, but he left before doing so. Would not the Master of the World order the creditors to wait until the *wazir* returns or else give orders for their claims to be met?" The "king" Dawlat-Shah, who was present, said, "Oh Master of the World, every day this man talks to us in Arabic, and I do not know what he is saying. Do you know, Nasir ad-Din?" He said this so that Nasir ad-Din might repeat what he had said. Nasir ad-Din answered, "He talks about the debt which he has contracted."

The sultan said, "When we return to the capital, go yourself to the treasury and give him this money." The treasurer was present and said "Oh Master of the World, he is very extravagant. I have seen him before in our own land, at the court of Sultan Tarmashirin." Alter this, the sultan invited me to his meal, I being in total ignorance of what had taken place. As I went out, Nasir ad-Din said, "Thank the king Dawlat-Shah", and Dawlat-Shah said to me, "Thank the treasurer."

The day after our return, I went to the palace, and presented to the sultan two camels with richly embroidered saddles and harness, along with eleven plates of sweetmeats. He ordered the sweetmeats to be taken into his private apartments and, on retiring to them, sent for me. After we had eaten, he asked me the names of the sweetmeats which he had particularly enjoyed, and thereafter we took betel and withdrew. A few moments, later the treasurer came to me and said "Send your friends to receive the money", so I sent them, and on returning to my house after the sunset prayer found the money there in three sacks, containing the fifty-five thousand dinars which was the amount of my debt, together with the twelve thousand which the sultan had previously commanded to be paid to me, less one-tenth according to their custom.

ON THE 9TH of first Jumada [October 1341], the sultan left Delhi for Ma'bar to fight with a rebel in that district. I was all prepared to accompany him, but was commanded with some others to remain in Delhi, and the chamberlain took written acknowledgments of the order from us as a proof that we had received it. The sultan also commanded that I should take charge of the mausoleum of Sultan Qutb ad-Din. He then sent for us to bid us farewell, and asked me if I had any requests. I took out a piece of paper with six petitions, but he said to me, "Speak with your tongue." Amongst other things, I said, "What shall I do about the mausoleum of Sultan Qutb ad-Din? I have given appointments in connection with it to four hundred and sixty persons, and the income from its endowment does not cover their salaries and food." He said to the *wazir*, "Fifty thousand" and then added, "You must have an anticipatory crop." This means, "Give him a hundred thousand maunds of wheat and rice to be expended during this year, until the crops produced by the endowments come in." I asked also that my house might be repaired. When I had been granted my requests, he said, "There is another recommendation, and that is that you incur no debts and so avoid being pressed for payment, for you will not find anyone to bring me news of them. Regulate your expenses according to what I have given you, as God has said [in the Koran] *Keep not thy hand bound to thy neck, neither open it to fullest extent* and again *Eat and drink, and be not prodigal.*" I desired to kiss his foot, but he prevented me and held back my head with his hand, so I kissed that and retired.

I returned to the capital and busied myself with repairing my house; on this I spent four thousand dinars, of which I received from the treasury six hundred and paid the rest myself. I also built a mosque opposite my house, and occupied myself with the dispositions for the mausoleum of Sultan Qutb ad-Din. The sultan had fixed the daily issue of food there at twelve maunds of flour and a like quantity of meat. I saw that this amount was too small, and that the produce which the sultan had put at my disposal was plentiful, and consequently I dispensed every day thirty-five maunds of flour and thirty-five of meat, together with proportionate quantities of sugar, candy, ghee and betel, not only to the salaried employees but also to visitors and travellers.

THE FAMINE at that time was severe, but the population were relieved by this food, and the news of it spread far and wide. The "King" Sabih, having gone to join the sultan at Dawlat Abid, was asked by him for news of the doings of the people and answered, "If there were in Delhi two such men as so-and-so there would be no complaints of famine." The sultan was pleased at this and sent me a robe of honour from his own wardrobe.

On setting out for Ma'bar, an epidemic broke out in the sultan's army, so he returned and built a camp near the river Ganges. I left Delhi and joined him there, and remained with him through the campaign against the rebel governor of Oudh. He gave me some thoroughbred horses when distributing them to his courtiers and included me in the number of the latter. I was present with him at the battle and capture of the rebel, and returned with him to Delhi. Afterwards, I fell into disfavour with him because I had visited the sheikh Shihab ad-Din in his cave outside Delhi. He had thoughts of punishing me and gave orders that four of his slaves should remain constantly beside me in the audience-hall. When this action is taken with anyone, it rarely happens that he escapes. I fasted five days on end, reading the Koran from cover to cover each day, and tasting nothing but water. After five days, I broke my fast and then continued to fast for another four days on end, and was set free after the sheikh's death, praise be to God.

SOME TIME LATER, I withdrew from the sultan's service and attached myself to the learned and pious imam Kamal ad-Din, "The Cave Man", as I have already related. The sultan was in Sind at the time, and at hearing of my retreat from the world summoned me. I entered his presence dressed as a mendicant, and he spoke to me very kindly, desiring me to return to his service. I refused and asked him for permission to travel to Mecca, which he granted. This was at the end of second Jumada 742 [early December 1341].

Forty days later, the sultan sent me saddled horses, slave girls and boys, robes and a sum of money, so I put on the robes and went to him. I had a tunic of blue cotton which I wore during my retreat, and as I took it off and dressed in the sultan's robes, I upbraided myself. Ever after when I looked at that tunic, I felt a light within me, and it remained in my possession until the infidels despoiled me of it on the sea.

When I presented myself before the sultan, he showed

me greater favour than before, and said to me, "I have sent for you to go as my ambassador to the king of China, for I know your love of travel." He then provided me with everything I required and appointed certain other persons to accompany me, as I shall relate.

The king of China had sent valuable gifts to the sultan, including a hundred slaves of both sexes, five hundred pieces of velvet and silk cloth, musk, jewelled garments and weapons, with a request that the sultan would permit him to rebuild the idol-temple which is near the mountains called Qarajil [Himalayas]. It is in a place known as Samhal, to which the Chinese go on pilgrimage; the Muslim army in India had captured it, laid it in ruins and sacked it. The sultan, on receiving this gift, wrote to the king saying that the request could not be granted by Islamic law, as permission to build a temple in the territories of the Muslims was granted only to those who paid a poll-tax; to which he added, "If thou wilt pay the *jizya* we shall empower thee to build it. And peace be on those who follow the True Guidance."

He requited his present with an even richer one - a hundred thoroughbred horses, a hundred white slaves, a hundred Hindu dancing- and singing-girls, twelve hundred pieces of various kinds of cloth, gold and silver candelabra and basins, brocade robes, caps, quivers, swords, gloves embroidered with pearls, and fifteen eunuchs. As my fellow ambassadors, the sultan appointed the amir Zahir ad-Din of Zanjan, one of the most eminent men of learning, and the eunuch Kafur, the cupbearer, into whose keeping the present was entrusted. He sent the amir Muhammad of Herat with a thousand horsemen to escort us to the port of embarkation, and we were accompanied by the Chinese ambassadors, fifteen in number, along with their servants, about a hundred men in all. We set out therefore in imposing force and formed a large camp. The sultan gave instructions that we were to be supplied with provisions while we were travelling through his dominions. Our journey began on the 17th of Safar 743 [22nd July, 1342].

8

DIEGO CHANCA - WITH COLUMBUS AT HISPANIOLA, 1493-94

*L*ittle is known about Dr Diego Álvarez Chanca *(unknown-1515), other than that he was a Spanish physician who was appointed by Ferdinand and Isabella, the King and Queen of Spain, to accompany Christopher Columbus on his second voyage west in September 1493. Chanca wrote a long, detailed letter to to the council of his native city of Seville, describing this expedition, the Caribbean islands and their inhabitants.*

Columbus (c.1451-1506), the Italian explorer, navigator, and coloniser, was the first European to explore the Caribbean islands and the mainland from Honduras to Venezuela and opened up the best routes to America (though he never set foot on, let alone discovered, North America). At the end of his first voyage, in January 1493, he left a settlement of about 40 Spaniards on the island of Hispaniola, in the hope they would find gold. He returned at the end of the same year with a fleet of of about 17 ships and 1,200 men, ready to be the second wave of colonists. They visited the islands of Dominica and Martinique, and explored Antigua, St Croix, and Puerto Rico, before returning to Hispaniola.

This edited extract of Chanca's letter explains the fate of that first settlement and details Columbus's determination to select another site for a second settlement and to colonise the island for Spain in order to capture all its gold. This would lead to the virtual enslavement of the island's indigenous Indian inhabitants and to a state of perpetual brutality and conflict. Within five years, two-thirds of the indigenous population would be wiped out.

~

'THE ADMIRAL ORDERED US TO GO ALONG THE UPPER COAST, BECAUSE WE'D BEEN GIVEN TIDINGS THERE WAS GOLD THERE'

WE RAN along the coast of this island for nearly a hundred leagues, thinking that within this range we should find the spot where the Admiral had left his men. That day, one of our sailors, who had been wounded in an affray with the Caribbees, died. As we were proceeding along the coast, an opportunity arose for a boat to go on shore to bury him, accompanied by two caravels to protect it.

When they reached shore, a great number of Indians came out to the boat, some wearing necklaces and earrings of gold, and asked to accompany the Spaniards to the ships; two of them were received on board with great kindness, and taken to the Admiral's ship, where, through the medium of an interpreter, they related that a certain king had sent them to find out who we were, and to invite us to land, adding that they had plenty of gold and provisions, to which we should be welcome.

The Admiral ordered that shirts, caps, and other trifles, should be given to each of the Indians, and told them that as he was going to the place where Guacamari dwelt, he would not stop then, but that there would be another opportunity of seeing him, and with that they departed. We continued till we came to an harbor called Monte Cristi, where we remained two days, in order to observe the character of the land; for the Admiral had objections to the spot where he had left his men with the view of making the first settlement.

We went on shore to see the land: there was a large river of excellent water close by; but the ground was inundated, and very ill-suited for habitation. As we went on making our observations, some of our men found two dead bodies by the river's side, one with a rope around his neck, and the other with rope around his foot. On the following day, they found two other corpses farther on, and one of these had a great quantity of beard; this was regarded as a very suspicious circumstance by many of our people, because all the Indians go beardless.

This harbor was twelve leagues from the place where the Spaniards had been left by the Admiral under the protection of Guacamari, the king of that province. After two days we set sail for there, but as it was late when we arrived there, and as there were some shoals, where the Admiral's ship had previously been lost, so we did not venture to put to shore, but remained at a little less than a league from the coast, waiting until the morning, when we might enter securely.

After we had anchored that night, the Admiral ordered two cannons to be fired, to see if the Spaniards who had stayed with Guacamari, would fire in return, for they also had cannons. But when we received no reply, and could not perceive any fires, nor the slightest symptom of habitation, our spirits became very depressed, and we began to enter-tain the suspicion which the circumstances dictated. While we were in this despondent mood, and when four or five hours of the night had passed away, a canoe came up, with the Indians onboard loudly asking for the Admiral.

They were conducted to the Admiral's vessel, but would not go on board till he had spoken to them, and they had asked for a light, in order to assure themselves that it was he who conversed with them. One of them was a cousin of Guacamari, who had been sent by him once before: it appeared, that after they had turned back the previous evening, they had been ordered by Guacamari to deliver two masks of gold as a present; one for the Admiral, the other for a captain who had accompanied him on the former voyage. They remained on board for three hours, talking with the Admiral in the presence of all of us. He showed much pleasure in their conversation, and inquired about the welfare of the Spaniards whom he had left behind. Guacamari's cousin replied that those who remained were all well, but that some of them had died of disease, and others had been killed in quarrels that had arisen amongst them; and that Guacamari was at some distance, lying ill from a wound in his leg, which was why he had not appeared, but that he would come on the next day.

He also said also that two kings, named Caonab and Mayreni, had come to fight with Guacamari and that they had burned the village. The Indians then departed, saying they would return on the following day with Guacamari. The next morning, we were expecting that Guacamari would come; in the meantime, some of our men landed on the command of the Admiral, and went to the spot where the Spaniards had formerly been: they found the building in which they lived burnt and levelled to the ground. They also found some cloaks and clothing. They observed, too, that the Indians who were near the spot, looked very shy, and dared not approach, but, on the contrary, fled from them. This appeared strange to us, for the Admiral had told us that during the former voyage, when he arrived at this place, so many came in canoes that there was no keeping them off; now that they were suspicious of us, it gave us a very unfavorable impression.

We threw trifles, such as hawk bells and beads, towards them, in order to conciliate them, but only four, a relation of Guacamari's and three others, took courage to enter the boat, and were rowed on board. When they were asked about the Spaniards, they replied that all of them were dead; we had been told this already by one of the Indians whom we had brought from Spain, and who had conversed with the two Indians that had earlier come on board with their canoe, but we had not believed it. Guacamari's kinsman was asked who had killed them; he replied that the king of Caonab and king Mayreni had made an attack upon them, and burnt the buildings on the spot, that many were wounded in the affray, and among them Guacamari, who had received a wound in his thigh. He also stated that he wished to go and fetch him; upon which some trifles were given to him, and he took his departure for the place of Guacamari's abode. All that day we remained in expectation of them, and when we saw that they did not come, many suspected that the Indians who had been on board the night before, had been drowned; for they had had wine given them two or three times, and they had come in a small canoe that might be easily upset.

THE NEXT MORNING, the Admiral went on shore, taking some of us with him. We went to where the settlement had been, and found it utterly destroyed by fire, and the clothes of the Spaniards lying about upon the grass, but found no dead bodies. There were many different opinions amongst us: some suspected that Guacamari was involved in the betrayal and death of the Christians; others thought not, because his own residence had been burnt. It remained shrouded in doubt. The Admiral ordered all the ground which had been occupied by the fortifications of the Spaniards to be searched, for he had left orders with them to bury all the gold that might be found. While this was being done, the Admiral wished to examine a spot at about a league's distance, which seemed to be suitable for building a town, and some of us went with him, making our observations of the land as we went along the coast.

We reached a village of seven or eight houses, from which the Indians fled when they saw us approach, carrying away what they could, and leaving the things which they could not remove, hidden amongst the grass outside the houses. These people build for themselves the most miserable hovels that can be imagined, and all the houses are so covered with grass and dampness, that I am amazed at the way they live. In the houses, we found many things belonging to the Spaniards, which it is unlikely they would have bartered, such as a very handsome Moorish mantle, which had not been unfolded since it was brought from Spain, stockings and pieces of cloth, also an anchor belonging to the ship which the Admiral had lost here on the previous voyage; this confirmed our suspicions.

On examining a closely woven and very secure basket, we found a man's head kept with great care; this we judged might be the head of a father, or mother, or of some person whom they much regarded: I have since heard that many were found in the same state, which makes me believe that this first impression was the true one.

When we returned to the site of the settlement, we found many Indians, who had regained their courage, bartering gold with our men. We also learned that they had shown where the bodies of eleven of the dead Spaniards were laid, which were already covered with the grass that had grown over them; and they all with one voice asserted that Caonab and Mayreni had killed them. Notwithstanding this, we also began to hear complaints that one of the Spaniards had taken three women to himself, and another four; from which we drew the inference that jealousy was the cause of the misfortune that had occurred. On the next morning, as nowhere in that vicinity appeared suitable for our making a settlement, the Admiral ordered a caravel to go in one direction to look for a convenient locality, while some of us went with him another way. In the course of our explorations, we discovered a harbor, of great security, and a very favorable situation for a settlement; but as it was far from where we wanted to have the gold mine, the Admiral decided to settle only in some spot which would give us greater certainty of attaining that aim. On our return, we found the other caravel, in which Melchior and four or five other trustworthy men had been exploring with a similar intention.

They reported that as they went along the coast, a canoe came out to them containing two Indians, one of whom was the brother of Guacamari. They said that Guacamari had sent them to ask the Spaniards to come on shore, as his settlement was near, with nearly fifty houses. The chief men of the party then went on shore in the boat, proceeded to the place where Guacamari was, and found him stretched on his bed, complaining of a severe wound. They conferred with him, and inquired about the Spaniards. His reply was, in accordance with the account already given by the others, viz. - that the men had been killed by Caonab and Mayreni, who also had wounded him in the thigh; which he showed to them bandaged up. On seeing this, they concluded that his statement was correct.

When they left, Guacamari gave each of them a jewel of gold. The Indians beat the gold into very thin plates, in order to make masks of it, and to be able to set it in bitumen; if it were not so prepared it could not be mounted; they make other ornaments of it, to wear on the head and to hang in the ears and nostrils; for these also they require it to be thin; since they set no store by it as wealth but only for adornment.

Guacamari desired them by signs and as well as he was able, to tell the Admiral that as he was thus wounded, he prayed him to have the goodness to come to see him. The sailors told this to the Admiral when he arrived. The next morning, he resolved to go there, for it could be reached in three hours, being scarcely three leagues distant; but as it would be the dinner-hour when we arrived, we dined before we went on shore. After dinner, the Admiral gave orders that all the captains should come with their barges. Then the Admiral went on shore accompanied by all the principal officers, so richly dressed that they would have made a fine appearance even in any of our chief cities. He took with him some articles as presents, having already received from Guacamari a certain quantity of gold, and it was reasonable that he should make a commensurate response to his acts and expressions of goodwill.

WHEN WE ARRIVED, we found Guacamari stretched upon his

hammock. He did not rise, but made the best gesture of courtesy of which he was capable. He showed much feeling with tears in his eyes for the death of the Spaniards, and began speaking on the subject, explaining to the best of his power, how some died of disease, others had gone to Caonab in search of the gold mine, and had been killed there, and that the rest had been attacked and slain in their own town. By the appearance of the dead bodies, it was less than two months since this had happened. Then he presented the Admiral with eight marks and a half of gold, and five or six belts worked with stones of various colors, and a cap of similar jewel-work, which I think they must value very highly, because it was presented to him with great reverence. It appears to me that these people put more value upon copper than gold.

The surgeon of the fleet and myself being present, the Admiral told Guacamari that we were skilled in the treatment of human disorders, and wished that he would show us his wound. He replied that he was willing; upon which I said it would be necessary that he should, if possible, go out of the house, because we could not see well on account of the place being darkened by the crowd of people; to this he consented, I think more from timidity than inclination, and left the house leaning on the arm of the Admiral. After he was seated, the surgeon approached him and began to untie the bandage; then he told the Admiral that the wound was made with a *ciba*, by which he meant a stone. When the wound was uncovered, we went up to examine it: it is certain that there was no more wound on that leg than on the other, although he cunningly pretended that it pained him much. Ignorant as we were of the facts, it was impossible to come to a definite conclusion. There was certainly a lot of proof a hostile people had invaded, and the Admiral was at a loss what to do; he with many others thought, however, that for the present, and until they could ascertain the truth, they ought to conceal their distrust; for after ascertaining it, they would be able to claim whatever indemnity they thought proper.

That evening, Guacamari accompanied the Admiral to the ships, and when they showed him the horses and other objects of interest, their novelty struck him with the greatest amazement. He took supper on board, and returned that evening to his house. The Admiral told him that he wished to settle there and to build houses; to which he assented, but said that the place was not wholesome, because it was very damp: and so it most certainly was.

All this passed through the interpretation of two of the Indians who had gone to Spain in the last voyage, and who were the sole survivors of seven who had embarked with us; five died on the voyage, and these two only narrowly escaped.

THE NEXT DAY we anchored in that port: Guacamari sent word to know when the Admiral intended leaving, and was told that he would do so on the morrow. The same day, Guacamari'sbrother, and others with him, came on board, bringing gold to barter; on the day of our departure also they bartered a great quantity of gold. There were ten women on board, of those who had been taken in the Caribbee islands, and it was observed that the brother of Guacamari spoke with them; we think that he told them to make an effort to escape that night; for certainly during our first sleep they dropped themselves quietly into the water, and went on shore, so that by the time they were missed they had reached such a distance that only four could be taken by the boats which went in pursuit, and these were secured when just leaving the water: they had to swim considerably more than half a league.

The next morning, the Admiral sent to desire that Guacamari would cause search to be made for the women who had escaped in the night, and that he would send them back to the ships. When the messengers arrived, they found the place forsaken and not a soul there; this made many openly declare their suspicions, but others said they might have removed to another village, as was their custom. That day we remained quiet, because the weather was unfavorable for our departure. The next morning, the Admiral resolved that as the wind was adverse, it would be well to go with the boats to inspect a harbor on the coast at two leagues distance further up, to see if the formation of the land was favorable for a settlement; and we went there with all the ship's boats, leaving the ships in the harbor. As we moved along the coast, the people manifested a sense of insecurity, and when we reached the spot to which we were bound all the natives had fled.

While we were walking about, we found an Indian stretched on the hillside, close by the houses, with a gaping wound in his shoulder caused by a dart, disabling him from fleeing any further. The natives of this island fight with sharp darts, which they shoot with straps in the same manner as boys in Spain shoot their little darts, and with these they shoot with considerable skill to a great distance; and certainly upon an unarmed people these weapons are calculated to do serious injury. The man told us that Caonab and his people had wounded him and burnt the houses of Guacamari. Thus we are still kept in uncertainty respecting the death of our people, on account of the paucity of information on which to form an opinion, and the conflicting and equivocal character of the evidence we have obtained.

We did not find the position of the land in this port favorable for healthy habitation, and the Admiral resolved upon returning along the upper coast by which we had come from Spain, because we had had tidings of gold in that direction. But the weather was so adverse that it cost more labor to sail thirty leagues in a backward direction than the whole voyage from Spain; so that, what with the contrary wind and the length of the passage, three months had elapsed when we landed. It pleased God, however, that through the check upon our progress caused by contrary winds, we succeeded in finding the best and most suitable spot that we could have selected for a settlement, where there was an excellent harbor and abundance of fish, an article of which we stand in great need from the scarcity of meat. The fish caught here are very singular and more wholesome than those of Spain.

9

FLORENCE DIXIE - HUNTING IN
PATAGONIA, 1878

F lorence Caroline Dixie (1857-1905), *a fearless poet, novelist, travel writer, war correspondent and feminist, was born into the aristocratic Queensberry family and, as her obituary in* The New York Times *put it, "'inherited the eccentricities as well as the cleverness possessed by so many members of it".*

Born Florence Douglas in Dumfries, Scotland, she was the daughter of Caroline Margaret Clayton, a General's daughter, and Archibald Douglas, the 8th Marquess of Queensberry.

As a child, she was a tomboy who sought to match her brothers in physical activities, whether swimming, riding, or hunting. She rode astride, wore her hair in a short boyish crop, and refused to conform to fashion when being presented to Queen Victoria. She and her twin brother James were particularly close, calling each other "Darling" (Florence) and "Dearest" (James).

Educated at a convent school, which she hated, she found some consolation in writing poetry; her childhood verses were published much later as The Songs of a Child, and other Poems, *under the pseudonym "Darling".*

In 1875, aged 19, Douglas married Sir Alexander Beaumont

Churchill Dixie, a Baron known as "Sir A.B.C.D." or "Beau". Though she was only five feet tall, and her husband 6' 2", she apparently became the dominant partner in the marriage.

Both shared a love of adventure and the outdoor life, and are generally considered to have had a happy marriage, despite Beau's habits of drinking and gambling, which caused dire consequences. The couple were said to have been called "Sir Always and Lady Sometimes Tipsy" by contemporaries. In 1885, Beau's ancestral home and estate at Bosworth had to be sold to pay off his gambling debts.

During her early life and travels, Dixie was an enthusiastic sportswoman, an intrepid rider and shot. Apart from travelling widely, in particular to South America and Africa (she was appointed a war correspondent by The Morning Post and sent to cover the Boer War), Dixie also played a major role in establishing the game of women's football, organising exhibition matches for charity. In 1895, she became President of the British Ladies' Football Club, maintaining that "the girls should enter into the spirit of the game with heart and soul".

In December 1878, two months after the birth of her second son, Dixie and her husband left their aristocratic life and children behind them in England and travelled to Patagonia. She was the only female in her group. She had debated going to elsewhere, but chose Patagonia because few European men, and no European women, had by then set foot there.

Her account of the trip, called Across Patagonia, was published in 1881. This edited extract covers a hunting trip and captures the spirit of a passionate and strong-willed Victorian adventuress.

∾

'Until you've tasted the juicy morsel that is the guanaco's 'fat-behind-the-eye', you've not lived'

WE NOW STRUCK NORTHWARDS, leaving Cape Gregorio,
which lay directly opposite our late encampment, at our
backs. I'Aria [one of the guides] having to keep the troop
together single-handedly, we had plenty to do to help him,
and in galloping after refractory horses, urging on the lazy
ones, and occasionally stopping to adjust packs, the time
passed quickly enough. We occasionally crossed tracts of land
covered with a plant bearing a profusion of red berries of the
cranberry species. They were quite ripe now, and we found
them pleasant and refreshing. The weather was, as usual,
sunny and bracing; and except that as yet we had not seen a
guanaco or given chase to a single ostrich, we had nothing to
grumble about. I'Aria told us that we were certain to meet
with guanaco on that day's march, so, with this assurance, we
comforted ourselves and kept a sharp look-out, eagerly scanning the horizon of each successive plain, and woe betide the
unfortunate animal that might appear within our ken. The
day passed, however, and a dark patch of beeches, which
stood near the spot where we were to camp that night,
appeared in view without our having seen either an ostrich or
a guanaco. Somebody found an ostrich egg though, and it
was carefully kept for dinner-time, for although it must have
been laid two or perhaps three months, there was still a possibility of its being tolerably good, as these eggs occasionally
keep till the month of April, six months after laying time.

    Towards sunset we arrived at a broad valley scattered
over with picturesque clumps of beeches, and bordered on
its far side by a thick wood of the same tree. I'Aria pointed

out a spot to us where he said there were some springs, by the side of which we were to camp, and thither we accordingly rode. But when we got there no springs were to be seen, and I' Aria said he must have mistaken the place. He suddenly remembered, however, that a conspicuous clump of beeches, some way up the valley, marked the right spot, so we turned in that direction. But again was I'Aria mistaken, and when - following various of his sudden inspirations - we had wandered about the valley in all directions for a considerable time without coming across these problematic springs, we began to think ourselves justified in presuming that I'Aria had lost his way, and in charging him with the same. He denied the accusation, however, with a calm and steady assurance, which, considering that all the time he was leading us about in aimless helplessness, would have had something rather humorous about it had our situation been a less serious one.

If we did not succeed in finding the springs, besides having to endure the torture of thirst ourselves, we should have to stop up all night to look after the horses, who would be certain to go off in search of water and get lost. It was rapidly getting dark too, and there were no signs of the arrival of any of the other guides, whose absence was a further confirmation that we could not be on the right track. As a last resource, we resolved to separate, and each go in a different direction in search of water, though I must say we had little hopes of success, it being known to us that beyond the springs in question there was no other water in that part of the country for a considerable distance. Hurling bitter but useless anathemas at I'Aria, who was now confidently pointing out a new spot as the "really" right one, we accordingly broke up, and having arranged to fire a shot as a signal, should any one of us find water, dispersed over the valley in all directions.

I had hardly skirted the beechwood for more than a minute or so when my horse suddenly neighed joyfully, and in an opening among the trees I saw two or three small pools of spring water. Overjoyed, I lost no time in firing off my gun, the report of which soon brought up all the others, who had not gone far. In justice to I'Aria, it must be said that for the last hour he had been wandering about close to where the springs lay, and his persistent denial of having lost his way was so far justified. Besides, as there was no trail of any description across the pampa over which we had that day ridden, it was really no easy matter to hit on the right spot immediately.

We had just set up the tents and made the fire when [the two other guides] Gregorio and Guillaume, at whose prolonged absence, now that we were at the springs ourselves, we had become rather uneasy, appeared with the mules. They had been delayed on the road by the packs getting undone. Francisco [a horseman and servant] too soon came up, and though he had been unsuccessful in the chase, he arrived in time to cook an excellent omelette for our dinners with the ostrich egg which turned out to be perfectly sound and palatable.

THE NEXT DAY was to be devoted to guanaco hunting, the want of meat having become quite a serious matter; our dogs were getting weak, and our stores, on which we had to rely solely for food, were disappearing in an alarmingly quick manner.

It is marvellous how the ordinary excitement of hunting is increased when, as in our case, one's dinner depends on one's success; and it was with feelings almost of solemnity, that early in the morning we selected and saddled our best horses, sharpened our hunting-knives, slung our rifles, and, followed by the dogs, who knew perfectly well that real earnest sport was meant, threaded the beechwood and rode up onto the plateau, where, according to the unanimous assurance of the guides, we could not fail to meet with guanaco.

I'Aria and Storer [a servant] having been left behind to look after the camp, our hunting-party numbered seven. In order to cover as much ground as possible we spread out in a line, extending over about two miles, and in this order we cantered northward from the valley, carefully scanning the plain, which stretched flat away for a good distance, but apparently as bare of guanaco as it was of grass. The weather, unlike that of the preceding day, was very cold, and a bitterly sharp wind blew right into our faces, making those of our number who had neglected to bring their greatcoats or furs very uncomfortable. This, however, was a trifling matter, if only those good guanacos would obligingly make their appearance! But evidently nothing was farther from their minds, and we rode over the plain, mile after mile, with hopes which, like the thermometer, were gradually sinking towards zero.

As time went on, the haze which bound the plateau at our approach solidified itself into an escarpment. In due time this was reached, and I rode up it, expecting to find another plain on its summit as usual. Instead, however, a broken, hilly country appeared in view, crossed in all directions by ravines. I looked eagerly about, but still no guanaco. Our line of advance, meantime, lost its order, owing to the changed nature of the ground, and frequently I lost sight of all my companions, as I descended into a ravine, or rode

round the base of some tall hillock; but it was never long
before I caught a glimpse of one or other of them again.

THE WIND GOT colder and colder, a white cloud crept up on
the horizon, and grew and grew, sweeping swiftly towards
me, till I suddenly found myself enveloped in a furious hail-
storm. I came to a standstill, and covered up my head to
protect myself from the hailstones, which were very large.
The squall did not last long, but when I looked up again I
found the whole country was whitened over, an atmos-
pheric freak having created a dreary winter landscape in the
middle of summer. Suddenly I started; close to me stood,
perfectly motionless, and staring me full in the face, a tall
guanaco. I was so startled and surprised that for the space of
a minute I sat quietly returning his stare. A movement of my
horse broke the spell.

The guanaco darted up the side of a hill like lightning,
and pausing a moment on its summit, disappeared. I meanwhile had unslung my rifle, and was off in pursuit of him.
Instead of climbing the hill, I rode quickly round its base,
and on the other side, as I had expected, I discovered my
friend looking upward, no doubt thinking I should appear
by the same road he had come. I had the selfishness, though
I am sure sportsmen will excuse it, to wish to kill the first
guanaco myself, and I was therefore by no means displeased
to find that my companions had not as yet perceived us.
With a beating heart, I dismounted and walked slowly
towards the guanaco, who, though he saw me coming, still
remained quietly standing. My weapon was a light rook-
rifle, but though an excellent arm, it did not carry more than
150 yards with precision, and I was now something over 180
yards from my prey.

He allowed me to advance till within the required distance, but then, to my disgust, just as I was preparing to fire, leisurely walked on another thirty or forty yards before he stopped again, watching me the while, as it seemed with an amused look of impertinence, which aggravated me considerably. I slowly followed him, vowing to fire the moment I was within range, whether he moved or not. This time I was more successful. The guanaco allowed me to come within about the necessary 150 yards. "Poor fellow!" I murmured generously, as I brought my rifle up to my shoulder and took aim just behind his. Only one step forward to make quite certain. Alas! I took it, and down I went into a hole, which in my eagerness I had not noticed, falling rather heavily on my face. In a second I was up again, just in time to see the guanaco bounding up a far escarpment, taking with him my chance of becoming the heroine of the day. There was nothing for it but to walk back to where I had left my horse, and see what had become of my companions.

I TOOK the same road the guanaco had taken, on the remote possibility of falling in with him again. Riding up the escarpment above referred to, I came on to a broad plain, and there an exciting chase was going on, in which, as it appeared, I was condemned to take the part of a spectator only.

At some distance, and going across my line of sight, was a guanaco running at full speed, closely followed by a pack of dogs, in whose track, but some ways behind, galloped three horsemen, whom I made out to be my husband, and brother, and Gregorio. The guanaco at first seemed to be losing ground, but it was only for an instant; in another he bounded away with ease, and it was apparent that as yet he was only playing with his pursuers. The pace soon began to tell on the dogs; the less speedy were already beginning to tail off, one of them, probably Gregorio's swift Pie-de-Plata, being far in advance of its comrades, and by no means to be shaken off by the guanaco, who had now given up any playful demonstrations of superiority, and had settled down to run in good earnest.

On, on they go - quarry, dogs, horsemen, will soon be out of sight. But what's this? The guanaco has stopped! Only for a moment, though. But he has swerved to the left, and behind him, a new dog and horseman have appeared on the scene, emerging, as if by magic, from the bowels of the earth. The chase is now better under my view. If some lucky chance would only bring the guanaco my way! The fresh dog is evidently discomforting him, and his having had to swerve has brought all the other dogs a good bit nearer to his heels. But on he goes, running bravely, and making for the escarpment, for in the hilly country below he knows he is at an advantage.

The dogs seem to be aware of this too, for they redouble their efforts, a splendid race ensuing. Suddenly another horseman appears on the plateau, and the unfortunate guanaco must again swerve to the left, a movement which, hurrah ! brings him almost facing towards where I am standing. That is to say, he must cross the escarpment at some point on a line between myself and the newcomer, the other horsemen, from the manner the race had been run, forming a circle in his rear, which debarred his escape in any other direction. Seeing this, wild with excitement, I dug my spurs into my horse, and flew along the edge of the escarpment, the horseman on the other side doing the same, in order to shut out the guanaco and throw him back on his foes behind. Seeing his last chance about to be cut off, he redoubled his efforts to get through between us. On, on we strain.

Nearer and nearer he gets to the edge of the plain, and already, with despair, I see that I shall be too late. But faster even than the swift guanaco, a gallant black hound has crept up, and in another instant, though the former dashes past me within a yard of my horse's nose and disappears over the side of the escarpment, the good dog has already made his spring, and, clinging like grim death to the guanaco's haunch, vanishes with him.

After them, in another instant, swept the whole quarry of dogs, and by the time I reined in, and got my horse down the steep ravine, they had thrown the guanaco, which Pie-de-Plata had brought to a standstill below; and Francisco, the horseman who had last appeared on the plateau, and at so opportune a moment, had already given the coup de grace with his knife.

ONE AFTER ANOTHER the other hunters gradually arrived, their horses more or less blown; and whilst pipes were lit and flasks produced, we had leisure to examine this, our first guanaco. Looking at his frame, his long, powerful legs, his deep chest, and body as fine-drawn almost as a greyhound's, we no longer wondered that guanacos run as swiftly as they do. Indeed, this one would have laughed at us, had he not been closed in as he was. The fur of the full-grown guanaco is of a woolly texture, and in colour of a reddish brown on the back, the neck, and the quarters; being whitish on the belly and the inner sides of the legs. The head closely resembles that of a camel; the eyes, which have a strange look on account of the peculiar shape of the eye bones, are very large and beautiful. A fair-sized guanaco weighs from 180 to 200 pounds.

Meantime, Gregorio having begun to cut up the guanaco, to our chagrin it was discovered to be mangy — a disease very common among these animals, probably on account of the brackishness of the water; and the meat being consequently unfit for food, we abandoned it to the dogs, who now made the first good meal they had had since we left Sandy Point. They were soon gorged to such an extent that they became useless for hunting purposes, and we had therefore to ride on, now relying solely on our rifles.

Gregorio had seen a herd of guanacos at the far end of the plain over which the chase had taken place, and thither we accordingly rode. After half an hour's galloping, we reached its limit, finding below a broad valley broken up into various depressions and hillocks. At the base of one of the latter we saw a small herd of guanaco, within range of which, by dint of careful stalking, we presently managed to come. Two fortunate shots brought a couple of their number down, and luckily both turned out to be quite healthy. Under the skilful manipulation of Gregorio and Francisco, in a marvellously short space of time they were cut up, and the meat having been distributed among our various saddles, heavily laden, we turned homewards.

The way back seemed terribly long, now that we had no longer the excitement of hunting to shorten the time; and it seemed quite incredible that we had gone the distance we had been, when, towards sunset, after a cold and weary ride, we at last stood on the edge of the plain which overlooked the valley where lay our home for the nonce.

The evening had turned out fine, the boisterous wind which had annoyed us so much in the daytime had died away, and the sky was now bright and clear. Through the branches of the beech trees I could catch a glimpse of our camp, with its white tents just peeping over the green bushes, and a thin column of blue smoke rising up into the air, pleasantly suggestive of warm tea and other comforts awaiting us.

Farther on, in the long green grass of the valley, which was now glowing under the last rays of the sun, were our horses, some grazing, others lying stretched out, lazily enjoying their day's respite from work, whilst the colts and fillies, as is their wont at sundown, were frisking about and kicking up their heels in all the exuberance of youth, unconscious as yet of heavy packs and sharp spurs. Whatever special character the peaceful scene might otherwise want was fully supplied by the picturesquely wild appearance of my companions, as, eschewing contemplation, and anticipating dinner, they rode quickly ahead towards the camp on their shaggy, sturdy horses, their bodies muffled in the graceful guanaco robe, and huge pieces of red raw meat dangling on either side of their saddles, followed by the blood-stained hounds, who seemed thoroughly tired after their hard day's work.

But whatever country one is in, whatever scenes one may be among - in one's own cosy snuggery in England, or in the bleak steppes of Patagonia - there is a peculiar sameness in the feeling that comes over one towards the hours of evening, and which inevitably calls up the thought, 'It must be getting near dinner-time.' Yielding to this admonition, which to-day was by no means less plain than usual, I quitted my eyrie and rode down to the camp.

When I got there I found preparations for an ample meal in full swing. Ingeniously spitted on a wooden stave, the whole side of a guanaco was roasting before a blazing fire, and in the pot a head of the same animal was yielding its substance towards the production of what I was assured would turn out an excellent soup. At dinner-time I was able practically to confirm this assurance; a better broth cannot be concocted than that obtained from such a guanaco head, with the addition of rice, dried vegetables, chilis, etc. But, at the risk of incurring the charge of digressing too much on the subject of eating, I must pay a tribute to the delicacy of a peculiar morsel in the guanaco, which we called "Fat-behind-the-Eye", and which is, in fact, a piece of fat situated as indicated by its name. The tongue and the brain are rare tit-bits, but they must yield in subtle savouriness to the aforesaid bonne-bouche. Having once tasted it, till the end of our trip, guanaco head formed a standing item in our daily messes, and whatever other culinary novelties we discussed, and they were as numerous as strange, "Fat-behind-the-eye" always retained its supremacy in our affections as the *ne plus ultra* of Pampa delicacies.

10

VASCO DA GAMA - DIFFICULT TIMES
WITH AN INDIAN KING, 1498

V asco Da Gama (c.1460-1524), was the first European
to reach India by sea. The Portuguese explorer's
discovery of an ocean route to India, in 1497-98,
marked a significant epoch in the histories of geographical exploration, colonialism and commerce. It confirmed the hypothesis of
a circumambient ocean, first posited by Hecataeus in the 4th
century BC. It diverted the profitable spice trade with the East,
which for ages had passed through Syria and Alexandria, into a
new channel. In consequence, Venice lost her monopoly, and
Lisbon became for a time the great spice-market of Europe. It also
opened the way for an age of global imperialism and for the
Portuguese to establish a long-lasting colonial empire in Asia.

The name of the author of this journal is not known, but is
thought to be one of the senior officers on board Da Gama's fleet.
The edited extract published here starts shortly after Da Gama's
arrival in India on May 20, 1498, at a place called Calicut (now
Kozhikode, in the southern Indian state of Kerala). During clas-
sical antiquity and the Middle Ages, Kozhikode was dubbed the
"City of Spices" for its role as the major trading point of Eastern

spices. Da Gama, who had the rank of Captain-Major, had been
trying to establish a relationship with Calicut's king (whom he
mistakenly thought was Christian, rather than Hindu), but that
was proving problematical, particularly as Arab traders,
concerned at the arrival of European rivals, sought to stoke up
tensions.

∽

'THE MOORS TOLD THE KING THAT WE WERE THIEVES, THAT
WE'D RUIN HIS COUNTRY, AND OFFERED HIM RICH BRIBES TO
KILL US'

ON TUESDAY, May 29, the captain got ready the following
things to be sent to the king [of Calicut], viz., twelve pieces
of striped cloth, four scarlet hoods, six hats, four strings of
coral, a case containing six wash-hand basins, a case of
sugar, two casks of oil, and two of honey. And as it is the
custom not to send anything to the king without the knowledge of the Moor, his factor, and of his *bale* [governor], the
captain informed them of his intention. They came, and
when they saw the present they laughed at it, saying that it
was not a thing to offer to a king, that the poorest merchant
from Mecca, or any part of India, gave more, and that if he
wanted to make a present it should be in gold, as the king
would not accept such things. When the captain heard this
he grew sad, and said that he had brought no gold, that,
moreover, he was no merchant, but an ambassador; that he
gave of that which he had, which was his own private gift
and not the King's; that if the King of Portugal ordered him
to return he would intrust him with far richer presents; and
that if King Caniolim would not accept these things he

would send them back to the ships. Upon this they declared that they would not forward his presents, nor consent to his forwarding them himself. When they had gone there came certain Moorish merchants, and they all depreciated the present which the captain desired to be sent to the king.

When the captain saw that they were determined not to forward his present, he declared that as they would not allow him to send his present to the palace, he would go to speak to the king, and would then return to the ships. They approved of this, and told him that if he would wait a short time they would return and accompany him to the palace. The captain waited all day, but they never came back. The captain was very wroth at being among so phlegmatic and unreliable a people, and intended, at first, to go to the palace without them. On further consideration, however, he thought it best to wait until the following day. As to us others, we diverted ourselves, singing and dancing to the sound of trumpets, and enjoyed ourselves much.

On Wednesday morning, the Moors returned, and took the captain to the palace, and us others with him. The palace was crowded with armed men. Our captain was kept waiting with his conductors for fully four long hours, outside a door, which was only opened when the king sent word to admit him, attended by two men only, whom he might select. The captain said that he desired to have Fernao Martins with him, who could interpret, and his secretary. It seemed to him, as it did to us, that this separation portended no good.

When he had entered, the king said that he had expected him on Tuesday. The captain said that the long road had tired him, and that for this reason he had not come to see him. The king then said that he had told him that he came from a very rich kingdom, and yet had brought him nothing; that he had also told him that he was the bearer of a letter, which had not yet been delivered. To this the captain rejoined that he had brought nothing, because the object of his voyage was merely to make discoveries, but that when other ships came he would then see what they brought him; as to the letter, it was true that he had brought one, and would deliver it immediately.

The king then asked what it was he had come to discover: stones or men? If he came to discover men, as he said, why had he brought nothing? Moreover, he had been told that he carried with him the golden image of a Santa Maria. The captain said that the Santa Maria was not of gold, and that even if she were he would not part with her, as she had guided him across the ocean, and would guide him back to his own country. The king then asked for the letter. The captain said that he begged as a favour, that as the Moors wished him ill and might misinterpret him, a Christian able to speak Arabic should be sent for. The king said this was well, and at once sent for a young man, of small stature, whose name was Quaram. The captain then said that he had two letters, one written in his own language and the other in that of the Moors; that he was able to read the former, and knew that it contained nothing but what would prove acceptable; but that as to the other he was unable to read it, and it might be good, or contain something that was erroneous. As the Christian was unable to read Moorish, four Moors took the letter and read it between them, after which they translated it to the king, who was well satisfied with its contents.

The king then asked what kind of merchandise was to be found in his country. The captain said there was much corn, cloth, iron, bronze, and many other things. The king asked whether he had any merchandise with him. The captain replied that he had a little of each sort, as samples, and that if permitted to return to the ships he would order it to be landed, and that meantime four or five men would remain at the lodgings assigned them. The king said no: he could take all his people with him, securely moor his ships, land his merchandise, and sell it to the best advantage. Having taken leave of the king, the captain returned to his lodgings, and we with him. As it was already late no attempt was made to depart that night.

ON THURSDAY MORNING, a horse without a saddle was brought to the captain, who declined to mount it, asking that a palanquin might be provided, as he could not ride a horse without a saddle. He was then taken to the house of a wealthy merchant of the name of Guzerate, who ordered a palanquin to be got ready. On its arrival, the captain started at once for Pandarani, where our ships were, with many people following him. We others, not being able to keep up with him, were left behind. Trudging thus along we were overtaken by the *bale* who passed on to join the captain. We lost our way, and wandered far inland, but the governor sent a man after us, who put us on the right road.

When we reached Pandarani, we found the captain inside a rest-house, of which there were many along the road, so that travellers and wayfarers might find protection against the rain.

The *bale* and many others were with the captain. On our arrival, the captain asked for a canoe so that we might go to our ships; but the *bale* and the others said that it was already late - in fact, the sun had set - and that he should go next day. The captain said that unless he was provided with a canoe, he would return to the king, who had given orders to take him back to the ships, whilst they tried to detain him - a very bad thing, as he was a Christian like themselves. When they saw the dark looks of the captain they said he was at liberty to depart at once, and that they would give him thirty canoes if he needed them. They then took us along the beach, and as it seemed to the captain that they harboured some evil design, he sent three men in advance, with orders that in case they found the ship's boats and his brother, to tell him to conceal himself. They went, and finding nothing, turned back; but as we had been taken in another direction, we did not meet.

They then took us to the house of a Moor - for it was already far in the night - and when we got there they told us that they would go in search of the three men who had not yet returned. When they were gone, the captain ordered fowls and rice to be purchased, and we ate notwithstanding our fatigue, having been all day on our legs.

Those who had gone in search of the three men returned in the morning, and the captain said that after all they seemed well disposed towards us, and had acted with the best intentions when they objected to our departure the day before. On the other hand, on account of what had happened at Calicut, we looked upon them as ill-disposed.

WHEN THEY RETURNED, the captain again asked for boats to take him to his ships. They then began to whisper among themselves, and said that we should have them if we would order our vessels to come nearer the shore. The captain said that if he ordered his vessels to approach his brother would think that he was being held a prisoner, and that he had been forced to give this order, and would hoist the sails and return to Portugal. They said that if we refused to order the ships to come nearer we should not be permitted to embark.

The captain said that King Camolin had sent him back to his ships, and that as they would not let him go, as ordered by the king, he should return to the king, who was a Christian like himself. If the king would not let him go, and wanted him to remain in his country, he would do so with much pleasure. They agreed that he should be permitted to go, but afforded him no opportunity for doing so, for they immediately closed all the doors, and many armed men entered to guard us, none of us being allowed to go outside without being accompanied by several of these guards.

They then asked us to give up our sails and rudders. The captain declared that he would give up none of these things: King Camolin having unconditionally ordered him to return to his ships, they might do with him whatever they liked, but he would give up nothing.

The captain and we others felt very downhearted, though outwardly we pretended not to notice what they did. The captain said that as they refused him permission to go back, they would at least allow his men to do so, as at the place they were in they would die of hunger. But they said that we must remain where we were, and that if we died of hunger we must bear it, as they cared nothing for that. Whilst thus detained, one of the men whom we had missed the night before turned up. He told the captain that Nicolau Coelho had been awaiting him with the boats since last night. When the captain heard this he sent a man away secretly to Nicolau Coelho, because of the guards by whom we were surrounded, with orders to go back to the ships and place them in a secure place. Nicolau Coelho, on receipt of this message, departed forthwith.

But our guards having information of what was going

on, at once launched a large number of canoes and pursued him for a short distance. When they found that they could not overtake him they returned to the captain, whom they asked to write a letter to his brother, requesting him to bring the ships nearer to the land and further within the port. The captain said he was quite willing, but that his brother would not do this; and that even if he consented those who were with him, not being willing to die, would not do so. But they asked how this could be, as they knew well that any order he gave would be obeyed.

The captain did not wish the ships to come within the port, for it seemed to him - as it did to us - that once inside they could easily be captured, after which they would first kill him, and then us others, as we were already in their power.

WE PASSED all that day most anxiously. At night, more people surrounded us than ever before, and we were no longer allowed to walk in the compound, within which we were, but confined within a small tiled court, with a multitude of people around us. We quite expected that on the following day we should be separated, or that some harm would befall us, for we noticed that our gaolers were much annoyed with us. This, however, did not prevent our making a good supper off the things found in the village. Throughout that night, we were guarded by over a hundred men, all armed with swords, two-edged battle-axes, shields, and bows and arrows. Whilst some of these slept, others kept guard, each taking his turn of duty throughout the night.

On the following day, Saturday, June 2, in the morning, the *bale* and others came back, and this time they "wore better faces". They told the captain that as he had informed the king that he intended to land his merchandise, he should now give orders to have this done, as it was the custom of the country that every ship on its arrival should at once land the merchandise it brought, as also the crews, and that the vendors should not return on board until the whole of it had been sold. The captain consented, and said he would write to his brother to see to it being done. They said this was well, and that immediately after the arrival of the merchandise he would be permitted to return to his ship. The captain at once wrote to his brother to send him certain things, and he did so at once. On their receipt, the captain was allowed to go on board, two men remaining behind with the things that had been landed.

At this we rejoiced greatly, and rendered thanks to God for having extricated us from the hands of people who had no more sense than beasts, for we knew well that once the captain was on board those who had been landed would have nothing to fear. When the captain reached his ship, he ordered that no more merchandise should be sent.

FIVE DAYS AFTERWARDS, the captain sent word to the king that, although he had sent him straight back to his ships, certain of his people had detained him a night and a day on the road; that he had landed his merchandise as he had been ordered, but that the Moors only came to depreciate it; and that for these reasons he looked forward to what he (the king) would order; that he placed no value upon this merchandise, but that he and his ships were at his service. The king at once sent word saying that those who acted thus were bad Christians, and that he would punish them. He, at the same time, sent seven or eight merchants to inspect the merchandise, and to become purchasers if they felt inclined. He also sent a man of quality to remain with the factor already there, and authorised them to kill any Moor who might go there, without fear of punishment.

The merchants whom the king had sent remained about eight days, but instead of buying they depreciated the merchandise. The Moors no longer visited the house where the merchandise was, but they bore us no goodwill, and when one of us landed they spat on the ground, saying: "Portugal, Portugal." Indeed from the very first they had sought means to take and kill us.

When the captain found that the merchandise found no buyers at that place, he applied to the king for permission to forward it to Calicut. The king at once ordered the *bale* to get a sufficient number of men who were to carry the whole on their backs to Calicut, this to be done at his expense, as nothing belonging to the King of Portugal was to be burdened with expenses whilst in his country. But all this was done because it was intended to do us some ill turn, for it had been reported to the king that we were thieves and were about to steal. Nevertheless, he did all this in the manner shown.

ON SUNDAY, the 24th of June, being the day of St John the Baptist, the merchandise left for Calicut. The captain then ordered that all our people should visit that town by turns, and in the following manner: each ship was to send a man ashore, on whose return another should be sent. In this way all would have their turn, and would be able to make such purchases as they desired. These men were made welcome by the Christians along the road, who showed much pleasure when one of them entered a house, to eat or to sleep, and they gave them freely of all they had.

At the same time many men came on board our ships to sell us fish in exchange for bread, and they were made welcome by us. Many of them were accompanied by their sons and little children, and the captain ordered that they should be fed. All this was done for the sake of establishing relations of peace and amity, and to induce them to speak well of us and not evil. So great was the number of these visitors that sometimes it was night before we could get rid of them; this was due to the dense population of the country and the scarcity of food. It even happened that when some of our men were engaged in mending a sail, and took biscuits with them to eat, that old and young fell upon them, took the biscuits out of their hands, and left them nothing to eat.

In this manner, all on board ship went on land by twos and threes, taking with them bracelets, clothes, new shirts, and other articles, which they desired to sell. We did not, however, effect these sales at the prices hoped for when we arrived at Mozambique, for a very fine shirt which in Portugal fetches 300 reis was worth 30 reis, and 30 reis in this country is a big sum. And just as we sold shirts cheaply so we sold other things, in order to take some things away from this country, if only for samples. Those who visited the city bought cloves, cinnamon, and precious stones; and having bought what they desired they came back to the ships. When the captain found the people of the country so well disposed, he left a factor with the merchandise, together with a clerk and some other men.

WHEN THE TIME arrived for our departure, the captain-major sent a present to the king, consisting of amber, corals, and many other things. At the same time he ordered the king to be informed that he desired to leave for Portugal, and that if the king would send some people with him to the King of Portugal, he would leave behind him a factor, a clerk and some other men, in charge of the merchandise. In return for the present, he begged on behalf of his lord [the King of Portugal] for a bahar of cinnamon, a bahar of cloves, and also samples of such other spices as he thought proper, saying that the factor would pay for them, if he desired it.

Four days were allowed to pass after the dispatch of this message before speech could be had with the king. And when the bearer of it entered the place where the king was, the king looked at him with a "bad face", and asked what he wanted. The bearer then delivered his message, as explained above, and then referred to the present which had been sent. The king said that what he brought ought to have been sent to his factor, and that he did not want to look at it. He then desired the captain to be informed that as he wished to depart he should pay him 600 xerafins [a coin worth three-fifths of a rupee], and that then he might go: this was the custom of the country and of those who came to it.

Diogo Dias, who was the bearer of the message, said he would return with this reply to the captain. But when he left the palace, some men followed him, and when he arrived at the house in Calicut where the merchandise was deposited, they put a number of men inside with him to watch that none of it was sent away. At the same time, proclamation was made throughout the town prohibiting all boats from approaching our ships.

When the Portuguese saw that they were prisoners, they sent a young negro who was with them along the coast to seek someone to take him to the ships, and to pass on the information that they had been made prisoners by order of the king. The negro went to the outskirts of the town, where there lived some fishermen, one of whom took him on board, for payment. This the fisherman ventured to do because it was dark, and they could not be seen from the city; and when he had put his passenger on board he at once departed. This happened on Monday, 13th August, 1498.

This news made us sad; not only because we saw some of our men in the hands of our enemies, but also because it interfered with our departure. We also felt grieved that a Christian king, to whom we had given of ours, should do us such an ill turn. At the same time, we did not hold him as culpable as he seemed to be, for we were well aware that the Moors of the place, who were merchants from Mecca and elsewhere, and who knew us, could ill digest us. They had told the king that we were thieves, and that if once we navigated to his country, no more ships from Mecca, nor from any other part, would visit him. They added that he would derive no profit from trading with Portugal, as we had nothing to give, but would rather take away, and that thus his country would be ruined. They, moreover, offered rich bribes to the king to capture and kill us, so that we should not return to Portugal.

All this the captain learnt from a Moor of the country, who revealed all that was intended to be done, warning the captains, and more especially the captain-major, against going onshore. In addition to what we learnt through the Moor, we were told by two Christians that if the captains went ashore, their heads would be cut off, as this was the way the king dealt with those who came to his country without giving him gold.

Such then was the state of affairs. On the next day, no

boats came out to the ships. On the day after that, there came an almadia, with four young men, who brought precious stones for sale; but it appeared to us that they came rather by order of the Moors, in order to see what we should do to them, rather than for the purpose of selling stones. The captain, however, made them welcome, and wrote a letter to his people on shore, which they took away with them. When the people saw that no harm befell them, there came daily many merchants, and others who were not merchants, from curiosity, and all were made welcome by us and given to eat.

On the following Sunday, about twenty-five men came. Among them were six persons of quality, and the captain perceived that through them we might recover the men who were detained as prisoners on land. He therefore laid hands upon them, and upon a dozen of the others, being eighteen in all. The rest he ordered to be landed in one of his boats, and gave them a letter to be delivered to the king's Moorish factor, in which he declared that if he would restore the men who were being kept prisoners he would liberate those whom he had taken. When it became known that we had taken these men, a crowd proceeded to the house where our merchandise was kept, and conducted our men to the house of the factor, without doing them any harm.

On Thursday, the 23rd, we made sail, saying we were going to Portugal, but hoped to be back soon, and that then they would know whether we were thieves. We anchored about four leagues to the leeward of Calicut, and we did this because of the headwind. We returned the next day towards the land, but not being able to weather certain shoals in front of Calicut, we again stood off and anchored within sight of the city.

On Saturday, we again stood off and anchored so far out

at sea that we could scarcely see the land. On Sunday, whilst at anchor waiting for a breeze, a boat which had been on the lookout for us approached, and informed us that Diogo Dias was in the king's house, and that if we liberated those whom we detained, he should be brought on board. The captain, however, was of opinion that he had been killed, and that they said this in order to detain us until they had completed their armaments, or until ships of Mecca able to capture us had arrived. He therefore bade them retire, threatening otherwise to fire his bombards upon them, and not to return without bringing Dias and his men, or at least a letter from them. He added that unless this were done quickly he intended to take off the heads of his captives. A breeze then sprang up, and we sailed along the coast until we anchored.

When the king heard that we had sailed for Portugal, and that he was thus no longer able to carry his point, he thought of undoing the evil he had done. He sent for Diogo Dias, whom he received with marked kindness, and not in the way he did when he was the bearer of Vasco's present. He asked why the captain had carried off these men. Diogo Dias said it was because the king would not allow him and his to return to the ships, and had detained them as prisoners in the city. The king said he had done well.

He then asked whether his factor had "asked for anything", giving us to understand that he was ignorant of the matter, and that the factor alone was responsible for this extortion. Turning to his factor, he asked whether he was unaware that quite recently he had killed another factor because he had levied tribute upon some merchants that had come to this country? The king then said: "Go you back to the ships, you and the others who are with you; tell the captain to send me back the men he took; that the pillar, which I understood him to say he desires to be erected on the land, shall be taken away by those who bring you back, and put up; and, moreover, that you will remain here with the merchandise." At the same time he forwarded a letter to the captain, which had been written for him by Diogo Dias with an iron pen upon a palm-leaf, as is the custom of the country, and which was intended for the King of Portugal. The tenor of this letter was as follows:

"Vasco da Gama, a gentleman of your household, came to my country, whereat I was pleased. My country is rich in cinnamon, cloves, ginger, pepper, and precious stones. That which I ask of you in exchange is gold, silver, corals and scarlet cloth."

ON MONDAY, the 27th, in the morning, whilst we were at anchor, seven boats with many people in them brought Diogo Dias and the other men who were with him. Not daring to put him on board, they placed him in the captain's long boat, which was still attached to the stern. They had not brought the merchandise, for they believed that Diogo Dias would return with them. But once the captain had them back on board, he would not allow them to return to the land. The pillar he gave to those in the boat, as the king had given orders for it to be set up. He also gave up, in exchange, the six most distinguished among his prisoners, keeping six others, whom he promised to surrender on the morrow, if the merchandise were restored to him.

On Tuesday, in the morning, whilst at anchor, a Moor of Tunis, who spoke our language, took refuge on board one of our ships, saying, that all he had had been taken from him, that worse might happen, and that this was his usual luck. The people of the country, he said, charged him with being a Christian, who had come to Calicut by order of the King of

Portugal; for this reason he preferred going away with us, rather than remain in a country where any day he might be killed.

At ten o'clock, seven boats with many people in them approached us. Three of them carried on their benches the striped cloth which we had left on land, and we were given to understand that this was all the merchandise which belonged to us. These three came to within a certain distance of the ships, whilst the other four kept away. We were told that if we sent them their men in one of our boats they would give our merchandise in exchange for them. However, we saw through their cunning, and the captain-major told them to go away, saying that he cared nought for the merchandise, but wanted to take these men to Portugal. He warned them at the same time to be careful, as he hoped shortly to be back in Calicut, when they would know whether we were thieves, as had been told them by the Moors.

On Wednesday, the captain-major and the other captains agreed that, in as much that we had discovered the country we had come in search of, as also spices and precious stones, and it appeared impossible to establish cordial relations with the people, it would be as well to take our departure. And it was resolved that we should take with us the men whom we detained, as, on our return to Calicut, they might be useful to us in establishing friendly relations. We therefore set sail and left for Portugal, greatly rejoicing at our good fortune in having made so great a discovery.

On Thursday, at noon, being becalmed about a league below Calicut, about seventy boats approached us. They were crowded with people wearing a kind of cuirass [armour consisting of breastplate and backplate fastened together] made of red cloth, folded, with weapons for the body, the arms and the head. When these boats came within the range of our bombards, the captain-major ordered us to fire on them. They followed us for about an hour and a half, when there arose a thunderstorm which carried us out to sea; and when they saw they could no longer do us harm, they turned back, whilst we pursued our route.

11

IDA PFEIFFER - IN THE SLAVE MARKETS
OF NEW ORLEANS, 1853

I da Laura Pfeiffer (1797-1858) was an ardent, intrepid and enterprising traveller who, after a long marriage and raising two sons, decided, in her mid-40s, to fulfil her long-held ambition to see the world. The books she wrote about her adventures were extremely popular and were translated into seven languages; the money she made financed further travel and more books. In all, she travelled nearly 20,000 miles by land and 150,000 miles by sea, and visited regions to which no European had previously gone, or where even the bravest men had found it difficult to make their way. She was a member of geographical societies of both Berlin and Paris, but not of the Royal Geographical Society in London due its ban on females.

In 1846, she set out on a tour of the world, which was not accomplished without great hardships and dangers. She and a companion were attacked by a knifeman on a road outside Rio de Janeiro; she held him at bay using a parasol despite being twice stabbed, and was only saved when strangers rode to her rescue. Visiting a tribe of cannibals in Sumatra who had earlier eaten two American missionaries, she won them over by making them laugh, saying, "Come, come, you will never have the heart to kill *and eat a woman, and an old woman like me, whose skin is harder than leather!"*

In Ecuador, she witnessed an eruption of the Cotopaxi volcano and survived being thrown from her mule into a river teeming with alligators. In 1855, at the age of almost 60, she became one of the few women to climb the 6,262 metre Chimborazo mountain in the Andes, the closest point on Earth to the moon.

She gathered specimens of flora and fauna during her travels, which she later donated to European institutions. Vienna's Natural History Museum holds her mammal collection from Madagascar, while other artifacts of hers are in the British Museum. She died in 1858, aged 63, from liver cancer. The account we publish here is taken from her visit to the United States in 1854.

∾

'THE CRIME OF TORTURING A HUMAN TO DEATH IS THOUGHT LESS HEINOUS THAN DRINKING AN IRREGULAR GLASS OF BEER ON A SUNDAY'

DURING MY STAY at New Orleans, I several times visited the slave-markets, as well as the place where they are sold by public auction. The principal auctions take place every Saturday, in a magnificent hall that will hold conveniently 500 or 600 persons, and which on the other days of the week is used for auctions of houses, lands, etc. All round the hall are tribunes, three feet high, on which the auctioneer and the poor creature he is to sell take their places; and the slaves are always dressed to as much advantage as possible, and placed so that they can be seen perfectly by all buyers.

The auctioneer reads a paper, stating their age, bodily constitution, etc, and setting forth their various virtues and capabilities. He then mentions the price, and the auction begins.

A young mother, with one child in her arms and another at her side, was put up when I was there, at 600 dollars, and the highest bid was 1280, which the seller declined, as too small a price by several hundred dollars. Girls of twelve or thirteen years of age I saw sold for about 600 dollars, and they looked up with cheerful pleased faces at their purchasers, and seemed delighted with their smart clothes. Very likely, poor little creatures, they regarded it as the "proudest day of their lives". To me, however, the scene was too painful a one to look at long, and I left the place.

At the slave-dealers, the slaves were waiting in court-yards for customers: they were well-dressed, and not doing any work; and as I wished to see them, I talked as if I were likely to make a purchase of a cook and a man-servant, and immediately the dealer rang a bell to summon the slaves, and placed them in two rows, the men on one side, and the women and girls on the other, and then began to describe and extol his wares. For a good cook he asked 1200 dollars, and for one that was, as he said, not completely trained, 1100.

These slave-dealers are, inconsistently enough, despised and avoided by everyone, so that they are almost excluded from human society. But since the gentleman slaveholder buys and sells slaves as well as the dealer, since he equally lives upon the labour of these poor creatures, and regards them equally as mere cattle, I am really at a loss to conceive on what ground he can regard the dealer as so much viler than himself. But society is full of these capricious distinctions.

In order to have an opportunity of judging of the condition of slaves on the plantations, I visited several of them, and at one - that of Mr Cook, near Donaldsville - I made some stay. I am, of course, like every person with the ordinary feelings of humanity not warped by early prejudice, an enemy to slavery; I regard it as a disgrace to our common nature, and hold that a willing owner of slaves can have no claim to the title of Christian, if indeed he has to that of man.

Hating slavery everywhere, I most especially detest it in a republican country, where people value so highly their freedom and equality of rights that they would think themselves justified in shooting anyone who should attempt to detract from them, but who yet thus openly set at nought every principle of religion and morality.

It was with these sentiments I went to visit the plantations, and therefore certainly with no disposition to look with particularly favourable eyes on the "peculiar domestic institution", as it is called; but I am bound in truth and candour to state, that on those I visited the slaves appeared to be by no means in the unhappy position I had imagined. This was especially remarkable on Mr Cook's plantation, perhaps because this gentleman and his wife are among the best and most benevolent of the planters; and even their youngest children seem to be imbued with the same kindly spirit. I noticed one of them, a little fellow of six years old, putting by at dinner-time a portion of everything that was given to him ; and when I asked him who that was for, he answered, "That's for a little negro girl that plays with us. She is not quite well."

The negro cottages on this estate stood apart from each other, and contained a large room, in which either a family or two or three unmarried people lived. Their beds were good, and provided with pillows and blankets, and even mosquito nets, and each had, at least, one table, several stools, and wooden tuba and other vessels. A very large cottage in the middle of the village is used for a nursery, where the young children are taken care of while their mothers are at work; it is under the management of a strong, lively-looking negress.

After a lying-in the mother is allowed four weeks to remain at home; and as long as the infant requires the breast, occupation is found for her near her cottage. There is even a hospital for the negroes, consisting of two spacious apartments; and a physician visits it once a week, or every day if necessary.

I went several times without any of the family to the negro village, and always found the people looking very comfortable. Many were sitting before their doors with a lump of white bread in their hands, and occasionally hot roast pork. At six in the evening they left off work, and came home merry and laughing to their supper - an abundant portion of meal prepared with maize flour, which was exceedingly good. When the meal was over, they went from one hut to another, gossiping and joking, and not seeming at all aware that their lot was so miserable a one as it is declared to be.

The house slaves appeared at Mr Cook's to have very easy places; I never saw that they were scolded, far less punished; yet I certainly took care to keep my eyes open, and I could not help thinking that if slavery were everywhere what it was here, it must be an incomparably better fate than that of many of our workpeople and peasants in Europe. The serfage of Russia is undoubtedly far more severe.

The Russian peasant is the slave of his master, the slave

of the government, the slave of every Jack in office, and not unfrequently of the common soldier also. He must give his labour without payment to the owner of the land; he must pay taxes to the government; he must submit to all kinds of ill-treatment, and even blows, from government and military officers; and with all this he must earn his own living; and nobody gives him a garment to wear, though his own should drop off in tatters, nor pays his taxes for him, nor offers him so much as a morsel of bread, if his little bit of ground fails to yield its produce.

Of his treatment just as terrible stories might be told as any that can be related of the American slaveholders; and for the services he renders, cuffs and kicks are often his only reward. If his wife or his daughter should attract the attention of his lord, woe be to her and the whole family if she resist his wishes. The Russian serf is bound to the soil on which he is born, and can only leave it by serving in the army twenty-five years; he has to labour in the making of roads and bridges, and in transporting goods and travellers, without receiving any compensation. No legal tribunal can be said to exist for him; for the very person against whom he would usually have to complain would sit as the judge in his own cause. He has not like the American slave, a master who, having purchased him at a high price, will at least provide for his physical welfare; and, on the whole, of the two lots, that of the Russian peasant is assuredly the worst.

THE GOVERNMENT of the United States is, however, unpardonable, for not doing more to ameliorate the condition of the slaves. The laws relating to them are bad and defective; and even these, little as they could do for them, are not put in execution. The Americans say: "The government would have enough to do, if it troubled itself with these things. It cannot turn spy, or do anything that might interfere with the liberty of American citizens." It seems to me, however, that the government does contrive to be informed of infractions of the law in other matters - to know which is the landlord who pours out an unlawful glass of beer on a Sunday, or who is the guest that drinks it, or when the Maine Liquor Law [prohibiting the use of any spirits] is violated; and it might, therefore, if it had a mind, keep a more watchful eye on transgressions of a much more serious character. But perhaps the crime of torturing a human being to death is thought a less heinous one than drinking an irregular glass of beer on a Sunday.

How do the Dutch authorities in India contrive to protect slaves so well? A despotic government can find means to ameliorate the condition of the unfortunate class robbed of the first of human rights; and a free State, with whose principles the very existence of a slave is, in the view of mere common sense, irreconcilable, not only permits and favours slavery, but does not attempt even to soften its character by good laws. In the United States, a slave cannot give evidence in a court of justice, nor, strange to say, even lay a complaint; and a man may lawfully be torn from his wife and children (when they are above thirteen), or children from their parents, and sold separately. What heart-breaking scenes must not this alone give rise to. Would that it were possible to subject the legislators to some similar fate, that they might learn a little mercy. Of hundreds of stories of the ill treatment of slaves by the whites, I will merely mention two or three from a book published in New York in 1839, and called *American Slavery as it is*.

Mr G, a tutor in the family of a planter who had the reputation of being a mild master, writes, in July, 1832, the following anecdote: "One morning, when breakfast was just over, and grace had been said, one of the children asked for some more syrup or molasses; a female slave in attendance put a portion on its plate, rather larger than usual, but not more than the child had often eaten before. But the master flew into such a violent passion with her that he sprang up, and holding her hands with one of his, he struck her with the other, till he at last sank down exhausted by his exertions; and then, observing that his hand was too weak, pulled off his shoe, and went on striking the poor creature with the heel. At last she began to scream, and tried to protect her head with her elbows; and thereupon the master called another negro, and commanding him to hold her hands, continued the beating with all his might, till the victim sank upon the ground", and Mr G, on whom she called for help, thought she must have died. She was able, however, to get up, and, going out, washed the blood off, and came back to continue her attendance, with her head, ears, and eyes so swollen, that no one would have known her. For such a trifle as this, the planter was not called to account at all.

THERE IS another story of a Mr Benjamin Jacob Harris, a slaveholder of Richmond, in Virginia, who was brought to trial for beating a negro girl of fifteen to death, while his wife made a piece of iron red-hot and burnt her in various parts of the body. The verdict in this case was "Died in consequence of an over-severe chastisement"; but the murderer was acquitted. Some years afterwards this same Harris killed another of his slaves, and was again acquitted, because no one had witnessed the deed but negroes.

A captain in the United States navy, being angry with

one of his negro boys, put him on a chair, tied his hands together with a rope, and hung him up to a beam, so high that he could only just touch the chair with his toes. The master then beat the boy in that position till he fainted, and very soon afterwards died. And this cowardly ruffian, too, was acquitted.

In Goochland, in Virginia, a superintendent of an estate tied one of the slaves to a tree, and, after beating him cruelly, put some straw round him and actually burnt him to death. In this case the criminal was not a white, but a coloured man; so, though he was not hung as he deserved to be, he was punished, but, as his victim had been only a slave, merely with some months' imprisonment. This book contains more than a thousand of such cases; so that one can scarcely help wishing the unfortunate negroes might one day combine and take signal vengeance on their oppressors.

In this book it is stated that a meeting was held by the slaveholders to discuss the question whether it was more profitable to keep slaves well, and so spare the capital expended in their purchase, or to overwork them and to wear them out in seven or eight years. Unfortunately, the vote was in favour of the latter method; and many slaves died in consequence of the immoderate labour to which they were subjected.

The law in South Carolina allows a master to work a slave fourteen hours a day in winter and fifteen in summer, whilst the convicts in the prisons are only obliged to labour on the average nine hours; but most Slave States have no law on this subject, and the planter may work his slaves to death as soon as he likes. Concerning the instruction of the slaves, the humane white man's law only interferes to forbid it. To teach a slave to read or write is a punishable offence;

so we see that in this case the law does not object to spying into private affairs.

Every effort is made to keep the negro on the same level of barbarism on which he, or rather his forefathers, stood when brought from Africa.

With respect to religious instruction, the law is silent; and some few of the planters' wives keep Sunday schools for their negroes, and read the Bible to them, besides teaching them to sing psalms and hymns - leaving them, I suppose, to reconcile for themselves the moral and Christian precepts they hear taught from the book, with those they see put in practice before them - no very easy task. Clergymen also go occasionally into the plantations and preach to the slaves, but must do no more.

ONE VERY STRANGE thing is to find that, while the whites of America degrade their negroes to the level of the brute, they are still constantly in the habit of confiding to them the most precious of their possessions, namely, their children. From a negro nurse their infants derive their first nourishment; she watches over their early childhood, and not unfrequently becomes the confidante of the growing girl; for all this the despised race is found perfectly adapted. But must not so close an intercourse with such rude and sensually disposed women as the negress have a very injurious effect on the minds of the children? Must not the moral sensibility of the girl or boy suffer greatly from the speech and example of these people? And is not this practice a piece of unaccountable thoughtlessness an entire forgetfulness of duty on the part of the parents? But they probably think as they were brought up themselves, so may their children be; and the practice of devolving thus their heaviest cares upon others is too convenient to be abandoned. That there are exceptional cases of parents not thus negligent it is hardly necessary to say.

I am very much inclined to think that the system of slavery, by the consequences it entails, in a great measure avenges itself on the whites themselves. Their children are accustomed to be constantly waited upon; it would be a kind of disgrace so much as to tie a string for themselves, or pick up anything they had let fall. The slave is the hand of the child; and it follows quite as a matter of course that the child becomes imperious, capricious, idle, and frequently malicious; loses all energy for action, almost even for thought, and, alas too often all kindly feeling also. A boy or girl brought up in the Slave States may be distinguished very disadvantageously from others who have been differently circumstanced; and it is needless to say how powerful through life is the education received in childhood.

The lot of the free negroes and coloured people is scarcely preferable to that of slavery, not even in the Free, much less in the Slave States. Partly by law, and partly from the absurd prejudices of these tolerant Christians, they are excluded from society, and belong to no class - neither to the slaves nor the citizens. They are the pariahs of the United States; and as if to enable them to feel still more deeply the degradation of their position, they are allowed to visit schools and receive education. This is really almost a refinement of cruelty, for by education ambition is awakened, and the free negro becomes acquainted with the rights of men only to know that he is excluded from them. The law does not allow him to become a citizen of any State, nor have a vote at any election; it will not receive him as a witness, nor suffer him to become connected by marriage with any white family. Must not such invidious distinctions and prohibitions have a tendency to embitter the feelings of these people towards the favoured classes?

And while it is the first duty of every government, whatever may be its name, to promote morality and good feeling amongst its subjects, it here does so much the reverse, that if a white man who has children by a coloured woman would wish to acknowledge them and give them the rights of children he may not do it; and if he wishes to retain the good opinion of his white fellow-citizens, he will not even educate them; should he, however, choose to sell the children, and the mother with them (no very uncommon occurrence), he may do so without forfeiting, in the esteem of the world, his character as a man of honour.

I often spoke with Americans on this subject, but could never get them to acknowledge that there was anything wrong in it; and they always concluded with saying that if the free negroes did not like their treatment, they might emigrate to Europe, or go back to their own country. And where is, then, their country? Is it Africa? Where they were not born, where their families do not live, where the people do not speak their language? Surely not. For fifty years no slave has been brought hither from Africa, and all the negroes now in the United States are born Americans, and are merely descended from Africans. America, not Africa, is their country; and in my opinion they have as good a claim to the name of American as the whites, who are descended from European immigrants; what is denominated their native country they often do not so much as know by name.

As for emigrating to Europe, who would give them the means? And what could they do in a quarter of the world already so much overpeopled as to send out every year 100,000 wanderers to all parts of the earth? In America there is still need of hands and heads; and it is to emigration the United States owe, in a great measure, the power and importance they have attained.

There are actually people here who maintain that the system of American slavery is very beneficial in its results to the natives of Africa. The free negroes, they say, are educated, instructed in religion, and then sent to the negro Republic of Liberia on the coast of Africa, where they may convert their countrymen, and perform the office of missionaries.

A wonderfully clever contrivance, no doubt; but what if these envoys should relate to their African converts how they have been treated by Christians in the country from which they have brought their Christianity; how they have been degraded to the level of beasts of burden, cruelly punished for the smallest offences, worn out with unrequited labour, and sometimes tortured even to death - how even when free, they have been despised, refused the commonest rights, hunted out of society, not allowed so much as to sit down at a table, or take a place in an omnibus, by the side of the lowest vagabond of a white, but shunned as if their touch was contagious - how far would all this go in inspiring respect and love for the Christian religion? It is almost a pity that there is not some country where we white Christians could enjoy the same benevolent treatment as the negroes in the United States; it would doubtless prove so highly beneficial to our religion.

12

FRANCIS PRETTY - PLUNDERING GOLD
WITH DRAKE OFF SOUTH AMERICA, 1579

Francis Pretty was a sailor from Suffolk, who served in a senior position and wrote detailed accounts of two separate circumnavigations of the globe, first with Francis Drake in 1577 and later with Thomas Cavendish in 1588. As these were piratical adventures of dubious legality, concerned chiefly with plundering treasure from wherever and whomever they could, these accounts were officially suppressed by Queen Elizabeth. While she revelled in the treasures her buccaneers brought back to her, she was anxious to avoid overly provoking Spain, whose ships and ports in South America were the victims of the raids. His diary of Drake's celebrated voyage around the world (the second circumnavigation of the world in a single expedition after Magellan's half a century earlier) while running rings around the Spanish, was not fully published until 1600.

The extent of Drake's looting during this trip was extraordinary. From one Spanish treasure ship he captured off the coast of Peru, he seized 25,000 pesos of gold, amounting in value to 37,000 ducats of Spanish money (about £7m by modern standards). From another, the Cacafuego, Drake took a dozen chests of coins, 80 pounds of gold and 26 tons of silver. Small wonder the Spanish branded him a pirate and nicknamed him "El Draque" ("The Dragon"). King Philip II is even said to have offered a bounty of 20,000 ducats for Drake's head - the equivalent of several million dollars today.

When Drake eventually returned home to Plymouth in 1580, having transversed the world and reputedly landed off the coast of California, claiming it for Queen Elizabeth, his vessel, the Golden Hind, was so weighed down with treasure it was in danger of sinking. Elizabeth's half-share of the contraband was greater than the Crown's annual income; delighted, she threw a celebratory dinner aboard the Hind and knighted him. Drake's other backers were said to have made a 4,700% return on their investment in piracy.

Drake's exploits made him extremely rich and a national hero. He would go on to other adventures, including having a major role in England's defeat of the Spanish Armada in 1588. He died of dysentery, aged around 56, in 1596 while anchored off the coast of Portobelo, Panama, in pursuit of more Spanish treasure ships. He was buried at sea there, in full armour, encased in a lead coffin. Despite several attempts to find it, his body has never been recovered.

≈

'WE SHOT HER THREE TIMES, AND ON BOARDING, FOUND GREAT RICHES: JEWELS, 13 CHESTS OF COINS, 80LBS OF GOLD, AND 26 TONS OF SILVER'

WE CONTINUED OUR COURSE, and on the 29th of November came to an island called La Mocha [off the coast of Chile], where we cast anchor; and our General, hoisting out our boat, went with ten of our company to shore. Where we found people, whom the cruel and extreme dealings of the Spaniards have forced, for their own safety and liberty, to flee from the main, and to fortify themselves in this island.

We being on land, the people came down to us to the water side with show of great courtesy, bringing to us potatoes, roots, and two very fat sheep; which our General received, and gave them other things for them, and had promised to have water there. But the next day repairing again to the shore, and sending two men a-land with barrels to fill water, the people taking them for Spaniards (to whom they use to show no favour if they take them) laid violent hands on them, and, as we think, slew them. Our General seeing this, stayed here no longer, but weighed anchor, and set sail towards the coast of Chile. And drawing towards it, we met near to the shore an Indian in a canoe, who thinking us to have been Spaniards, came to us and told us, that at a place called Santiago, there was a great Spanish ship laden from the kingdom of Peru; for which good news our General gave him diverse trifles. Whereof he was glad, and went along with us and brought us to the place, which is called the port of Valparaiso.

When we came thither we found, indeed, the ship riding at anchor, having in her eight Spaniards and three negroes; who, thinking us to have been Spaniards, and their friends, welcomed us with a drum, and made ready a *botija* of wine of Chile to drink to us. But as soon as we were entered, one of our company called Thomas Moon began to lay about him, and struck one of the Spaniards, and said unto him, *Abaxo, perro!* that is in English "Go down, dog!". One of these Spaniards, seeing persons of that quality in those seas, all to crossed and blessed himself. But, to be short, we stowed them under hatches, all save one Spaniard, who suddenly and desperately leapt overboard into the sea, and swam ashore to the town of Santiago, to give them warning of our arrival.

They of the town, being not above nine households, presently fled away and abandoned the town. Our General manned his boat and the Spanish ship's boat, and went to the town; and, being come to it, we rifled it, and came to a small chapel, which we entered, and found therein a silver chalice, two cruets, and one altar-cloth, the spoil whereof our General gave to Master Fletcher, his minister.

We found also in this town a warehouse stored with wine of Chile and many boards of cedar-wood; all which wine we brought away with us, and certain of the boards to burn for firewood. And so, being come aboard, we departed the haven, having first set all the Spaniards on land, saving one John Griego, a Greek born, whom our General carried with him as pilot to bring him into the haven of Lima. When we were at sea our General rifled the ship, and found in her good store of the wine of Chile, and 25,000 pesos of very pure and fine gold of Valdivia, amounting in value to 37,000 ducats of Spanish money, and above. So, going on our course, we arrived next at a place called Coquimbo, where our General sent fourteen of his men on land to fetch water. But they were espied by the Spaniards, who came with 300 horsemen and 200 footmen, and slew one of our men with a piece. The rest came aboard in safety, and the Spaniards departed. We went on shore again and buried our man, and the Spaniards came down again with a flag of truce; but we set sail, and would not trust them.

From hence we went to a certain port called Tarapaca; where, being landed, we found by the sea side a Spaniard lying asleep, who had lying by him thirteen bars of silver, which weighed 4,000 ducats Spanish. We took the silver and left the man. Not far from hence, going on land for fresh water, we met with a Spaniard and an Indian boy driving eight llamas, or sheep of Peru, which are as big as asses; every of which sheep had on his back two bags of leather, each bag containing 50lb weight of fine silver. So that, bringing both the sheep and their burden to the ships, we found in all the bags eight hundred weight of silver.

From here we sailed to a place called Arica; and, entering the port, we found there three small barks, which we rifled, and found in one of them fifty-seven wedges of silver, each of them weighing about 20lb weight, and every of these wedges were of the fashion and bigness of a brick-bat. In all these three barks, we found not one person. For they, mistrusting no strangers, were all gone a-land to the town, which consists of about twenty houses; which we would have ransacked if our company had been better and more in number. But our General, content with the spoil of the ships, left the town and put off again to sea, and set sail for Lima, and, by the way, met with a small bark, which he boarded, and found in her good store of linen cloth. Whereof taking some quantity, he let her go.

To Lima we came the 13th of February; and, entering the haven, we found there about twelve ships lying fast moored at an anchor, having all their sails carried on shore; for the masters and merchants were here most secure, having never been assaulted by enemies, and at this time feared the approach of none such as we were. Our General rifled these ships, and found in one of them a chest full of reals [coins] of plate, and good store of silks and linen cloth; and took the chest into his own ship, and good store of the silks and linen. In which ship he had news of another ship called the Cacafuego, which was gone towards Payta, and that the same ship was laden with treasure. Whereupon we stayed no longer here, but, cutting all the cables of the ships in the haven, we let them go where they would, either to sea or to the shore; and with all speed we followed the Cacafuego toward Payta, thinking there to have found her. But before we arrived there she was gone from thence towards Panama; whom our General still pursued, and by the way met with a bark laden with ropes and tackle for ships, which he boarded and searched, and found in her 80lb weight of gold, and a crucifix of gold with goodly great emeralds set in it, which he took, and some of the cordage also for his own ship. From hence we departed, still following the Cacafuego; and our General promised our company that whosoever should first spot her should have his chain of gold for his good news. It fortuned that John Drake, going up into the top, saw her about three o'clock. And about six of the clock we came to her and boarded her, and shot at her three pieces of ordnance, and strake down her mizen; and, being entered, we found in her great riches, as jewels and precious stones, thirteen chests full of reals of plate, fourscore pound weight of gold, and six-and-twenty ton of silver.

The place where we took this prize was called Cape de San Francisco, about 150 leagues [south] from Panama. The pilot's name of this ship was Francisco; and amongst other plate that our General found in this ship he found two very fair gilt bowls of silver, which were the pilot's. To whom our General said, "Senor Pilot, you have here two silver cups, but I must needs have one of them; which the pilot, because he could not otherwise choose, yielded unto, and gave the other to the steward of our General's ships. When this pilot departed from us, his boy said thus unto our General: 'Captain, our ship shall be called no more the Cacafuego, but the Cacaplata, and your ship shall be called the Cacafuego.'"

Which pretty speech of the pilot's boy ministered matter of laughter to us, both then and long after.

When our General had done what he would with this Cacafuego, he cast her off, and we went on our course still towards the west; and not long after met with a ship laden with linen cloth and fine China dishes of white earth, and great store of China silks, of all which things we took as we listed. The owner himself of this ship was in her, who was a Spanish gentleman, from whom our General took a falcon of gold, with a great emerald in the breast thereof; and the pilot of the ship he took also with him, and so cast the ship off.

This pilot brought us to the haven of Guatulco, a town which, as he told us, had but 17 Spaniards in it. As soon as we were entered this haven, we landed, and went presently to the town and to the town-house; where we found a judge sitting in judgment, being associated with three other officers, upon three negroes that had conspired to burn of the town. Both which judges and prisoners we took, and brought them a-shipboard, and caused the chief judge to write his letter to the town to command all the townsmen to avoid, that we might safely water there. Which being done, and they departed, we ransacked the town; and in one house we found a pot, of the quantity of a bushel, full of reals of plate, which we brought to our ship. And here one Thomas Moon, one of our company, took a Spanish gentleman as he was flying out of the town; and, searching him, he found a chain of gold about him, and other jewels, which he took, and so let him go.

At this place our General, among other Spaniards, set ashore his Portugal pilot which he took at the islands of Cape Verde out of a ship of St Mary port, of Portugal. And having set them ashore we departed hence, and sailed to the island of Canno; where our General landed, and brought to shore his own ship, and discharged her, mended and graved her, and furnished our ship with water and wood sufficiently. And while we were here we espied a ship and set sail after her, and took her, and found in her two pilots and a Spanish governor, going for the islands of the Philippines. We searched the ship, and took some of her merchandises, and so let her go.

Our General at this place and time, thinking himself, both in respect of his private injuries received from the Spaniards, as also of their contempts and indignities offered to our country and prince in general, sufficiently satisfied and revenged; and supposing that her Majesty at his return would rest contented with this service, purposed to continue no longer upon the Spanish coast, but began to consider and to consult of the best way home.

13

SAMUEL DE CHAMPLAIN - THE
FOUNDING OF 'NEW FRANCE', 1609

S *amuel de Champlain (c.1567-1635) was a French explorer*
who founded the city of Quebec and mapped the Atlantic
coast and the Great Lakes. He was the first European to
have discovered the lake that bears his name and straddles the
border of America and Canada, and made other explorations of
what are now northern New York state, the Ottawa River, and
the eastern Great Lakes.

Champlain wrote extensively of his voyages and later life, but
little is known of his childhood. His earliest travels were with his
uncle, in 1601, venturing as far as Central America and the West
Indies. Such were his skills as a navigator that he soon gained an
honorary place at the court of Henry IV. In 1603, he joined the
first of many expeditions to colonise what was called New France
(present-day Canada). Champlain survived three winters there,
but scurvy killed most of his companions.

It was during a later expedition, in 1608, that Champlain
undertook the founding of Quebec, as leader of 32 colonists. They
erected a fort, with three main wooden buildings, surrounded by
a moat.This was the very beginning of the city. Champlain and
just eight others survived that first winter at Quebec, and were

bolstered by more colonists the following summer. Making allies with some of the local Indian tribes, Champlain joined them in defeating Iroquois marauders in a battle near the lake he named after himself. This and a similar victory in 1610 enhanced the position of the French colonists and the trade in fur between them and the Indians. In that year, he left for France, where he married Hélène Boullé, the daughter of the secretary to the king's chamber.

When fur trade later ran into financial trouble, Champlain persuaded Louis XIII to intervene. Eventually the king appointed a viceroy, who made Champlain commandant of New France.

In 1615, Champlain, 10 French soldiers and 300 allied Huron Indians took part in another military expedition against the Iroquois. The assault failed and Champlain was wounded twice in the leg by arrows, and, after retreating, was forced to spend the winter with the Huron. During his stay, he went on a great deer hunt, on which he became lost and was forced to wander for three days living off game and sleeping under trees until he was rescued by chance. He spent the rest of the winter learning "their country, their manners, customs, modes of life".

Champlain died from a stroke, aged 56, in Quebec. He would later be immortalised as the "Father of New France", and many places, streets, and buildings in north-eastern North America bear his name.

The edited extract published here is taken from one of his many books, and concerns that first battle with the Iroquois, in 1609.

≈

'THESE SOOTHSAYERS, OUT OF A HUNDRED WORDS, DO NOT SPEAK TWO THAT ARE TRUE'

I SET out accordingly from the fall of the Iroquois River on the 2nd of July. All the savages set to carrying their canoes, arms, and baggage overland, some half a league, in order to pass by the violence and strength of the fall, which was speedily accomplished. Then they put them all in the water again, two men in each with the baggage; and they caused one of the men of each canoe to go by land some three leagues, the extent of the fall, which is not, however, so violent here as at the mouth, except in some places, where rocks obstruct the river, which is not broader than three hundred or four hundred paces.

After we had passed the fall, which was attended with difficulty, all the savages, who had gone by land over a good path and level country, re-embarked in their canoes. My men went also by land; but I went in a canoe. There were twenty-four canoes, with sixty men. After the review was completed, we continued our course to an island, three leagues long, filled with the finest pines I had ever seen. Here they went hunting, and captured some wild animals. Proceeding about three leagues farther on, we made a halt, in order to rest the coming night.

They all at once set to work, some to cut wood, and others to obtain the bark of trees to cover their cabins, for the sake of sheltering themselves, others to fell large trees for constructing a barricade on the river-bank around their cabins, which they do so quickly that in less than two hours so much is accomplished that five hundred of their enemies would find it very difficult to dislodge them without being killed in large numbers. They make no barricade on the riverbank, where their canoes are drawn up, in order that they may be able to embark, if occasion requires. After they were established in their cabins, they despatched three canoes, with nine good men, according to their custom in all their encampments, to reconnoitre for a distance of two or three leagues, to see if they can perceive anything, after which they return. They rest the entire night, depending upon the observation of these scouts, which is a very bad custom among them; for they are sometimes while sleeping surprised by their enemies, who slaughter them before they have time to get up and prepare for defence.

Noticing this, I remonstrated with them, and told them that they ought to keep watch, as they had seen us do every night, and have men on the lookout, in order to listen and see whether they perceived anything, and that they should not live in such a manner like beasts. They replied that they could not keep watch, and that they worked enough in the daytime, since, when engaged in war, they divide their troops into three parts: namely, a part for hunting scattered in several places; another to constitute the main body of their army, which is always under arms; and the third to act as *avant-coureurs*, to look out along the rivers, and observe whether they can see any mark or signal showing where their enemies or friends have passed. This they ascertain by certain marks which the chiefs of different tribes make known to each other; but, these not continuing always the same, they inform themselves from time to time of changes, by which means they ascertain whether they are enemies or friends who have passed. The hunters never hunt in advance of the main body, or the *avant-coureurs*, so as not to excite alarm or produce disorder, but in the rear and in the direction from which they do not anticipate their enemy. Thus they advance until they are within two or three days march of their enemies, when they proceed by night stealthily and all in a body, except the *avant-coureurs*.

By day, they withdraw into the interior of the woods, where they rest, without straying off, neither making any noise nor any fire, even for the sake of cooking, so as not to be noticed in case their enemies should accidently pass by. They eat baked Indian meal, which they soak in water, when it becomes a kind of porridge. They provide themselves with such meal to meet their wants, when they are near their enemies, or when retreating after a charge, in which case they are not inclined to hunt, retreating immediately.

IN ALL THEIR ENCAMPMENTS, they have their *Pilotois*, or *Ostemoy*, people who play the part of soothsayers, in whom these people have faith. One of these builds a cabin, surrounds it with small pieces of wood, and covers it with his robe: after it is built, he places himself inside, so as not to be seen at all, when he seizes and shakes one of the posts of his cabin, muttering some words between his teeth, by which he says he invokes the devil, who appears to him in the form of a stone, and tells him whether they will meet their enemies and kill many of them. This *Pilotois* lies prostrate on the ground, motionless, only speaking with the devil: suddenly, he rises to his feet, talking, and tormenting himself in such a manner that, although naked, he is all of a perspiration.

All the people surround the cabin, seated on their buttocks. They frequently told me that the shaking of the cabin, which I saw, came from the devil, who made it move, and not the man inside, although I could see the contrary; for, as I have stated above, it was the *Pilotois* who took one of the supports of the cabin, and made it move in this manner. They told me also that I should see fire come out from the top, which I did not see at all. These rogues counterfeit also their voice, so that it is heavy and clear, and speak in a language unknown to the other savages. The savages think that the devil is speaking, and telling them what is to happen in their war, and what they must do.

But all these soothsayers, out of a hundred words, do not speak two that are true, and impose upon these poor people. There are enough like them in the world, who take food from the mouths of the people by their impostures, as these worthies do. I often remonstrated with the people, telling them that all they did was sheer nonsense, and that they ought not to put confidence in them.

Now, after ascertaining from their soothsayers what is to be their fortune, the chiefs take sticks a foot long, and as many as there are soldiers. They take others, somewhat larger, to indicate the chiefs. Then they go into the wood, and seek out a level place, five or fix feet square, where the chief, as sergeant-major, puts all the sticks in such order as seems to him best. Then he calls all his companions, who come all armed; and he indicates to them the rank and order they are to observe in battle with their enemies.

All the savages watch carefully this proceeding, observing attentively the outline which their chief has made with the sticks. Then they go away, and set to placing themselves in such order as the sticks were in, when they mingle with each other, and return again to their proper order, which manoeuvre they repeat two or three times, and at all their encampments, without needing a sergeant to keep them in the proper order, which they are able to keep accurately without any confusion. This is their rule in war.

WE SET out on the next day, continuing our course in the river as far as the entrance of the lake. There are many pretty islands here, low, and containing very fine woods and meadows, with abundance of fowl and such animals of the chase as stags, fallow-deer, fawns, roe-bucks, bears, and others, which go from the mainland to these islands. We captured a large number of these animals. There are also many beavers, not only in this river, but also in numerous other little ones that flow into it. These regions, although they are pleasant, are not inhabited by any savages, on account of their wars; but they withdraw as far as possible from the riversinto the interior, in order not to be suddenly surprised.

The next day, we entered the lake, which is large, say eighty or a hundred leagues long, where I saw four fine islands, ten, twelve, and fifteen leagues long, which were formerly inhabited by the savages, like the River of the Iroquois; but they have been abandoned since the wars of the savages. There are also many rivers falling into the lake, bordered by many fine trees of the same kinds as those we have in France, with many vines finer than any I have seen in any other place; also many chestnut-trees on the border of this lake, which I had not seen before. There is also a great abundance of fish, of many varieties: among others, one called by the savages of the country *Chaousarou*, which varies in length, the largest being, as the people told me, eight or ten feet long. I saw some five feet long, which were as large as my thigh; the head being as big as my two fists, with a snout two feet and a half long, and a double row of very sharp and dangerous teeth. Its body is, in shape, much like that of a pike; but it is armed with scales so strong that a *poniard* could not pierce them. Its color is silver-gray. The extremity of its snout is like that of a swine.

This fish makes war upon all others in the lakes and rivers. It also possesses remarkable dexterity, as these people informed me, which is exhibited in the following manner. When it wants to capture birds, it swims in among the rushes, or reeds, which are found on the banks of the lake in several places, where it puts its snout out of water and keeps perfectly still: so that, when the birds come and light on its snout, supposing it to be only the stump of a tree, it adroitly closes it, which it had kept ajar, and pulls the birds by the feet down under water. The savages gave me the head of one of them, of which they make great account, saying that, when they have a headache, they bleed themselves with the teeth of this fish on the spot where they suffer pain, and it suddenly passes away.

Continuing our course over this lake on the western side, I noticed some very high mountains on the eastern side, on the top of which there was snow. I asked whether these localities were inhabited, and was told that the Iroquois dwelt there, and that there were beautiful valleys in these places, with plains productive in grain, such as I had eaten in this country, together with many kinds of fruit without limit. They said also that the lake extended near mountains, some twenty-five leagues distant from us, as I judge. I saw, on the south, other mountains, no less high than the first, but without any snow. The savages told me that these mountains were thickly settled, and that it was there we were to find their enemies; but that it was necessary to pass a fall in order to go there (which I afterwards saw), when we should enter another lake, nine or ten leagues long. After reaching the end of the lake, we should have to go, they said, two leagues by land, and pass through a river flowing into the sea on the Norumbegue coast, whither it took them only two 66ys to go by canoe, as I have since ascertained from some prisoners we captured, who gave me minute information in regard to all they had

personal knowledge of, through some Algonquin inter-
preters, who understood the Iroquois language.

Now, as we began to approach within two or three days'
journey of the home of their enemies, we advanced only at
night, resting during the day. But they did not fail to practise
constantly their accustomed superstitions, in order to ascertain what was to be the result of their undertaking; and they
often asked me if I had had a dream, and seen their
enemies, to which Ireplied in the negative. Yet I did not
cease to encourage them, and inspire in them hope.

When night came, we set out on the journey until the
next day, when we withdrew into the interior of the forest,
and spent the rest of the day there. About ten or eleven
o'clock, after taking a little walk about our encampment, I
retired. While sleeping, I dreamed that I saw our enemies,
the Iroquois, drowning in the lake near a mountain, within
sight. When I expressed a wish to help them, our allies told
me we must let them all die, and that they were of no importance. When I awoke, they did not fail to ask me, as usual, if
I had had a dream. I told them that I had, in fact, had one.
This, upon being related, gave them so much confidence
that they did not doubt any longer that good was to happen
to them.

When it was evening, we embarked in our canoes to
continue our course; and, as we advanced very quietly and
without making any noise, we met on the 29th of the month
the Iroquois, about ten o'clock at evening, at the extremity of
a cape which extends into the lake on the western bank.
They had come to fight. We both began to utter loud cries,
all getting their arms in readiness. We withdrew out on the
water, and the Iroquois went on shore, where they drew up

all their canoes close to each other and began to fell trees with poor axes, which they acquire in war sometimes, using also others of stone. Thus they barricaded themselves very well.

Our forces also passed the entire night, their canoes being drawn up close to each other, and fastened to poles, so that they might not get separated, and that they might be all in readiness to fight, if occasion required. We were out upon the water, within arrow range of their barricades. When they were armed and in array, they despatched two canoes by themselves to the enemy to inquire if they wished to fight, to which the latter replied that they wanted nothing else; but they said that, at present, there was not much light, and that it would be necessary to wait for daylight, so as to be able to recognize each other; and that, as soon as the sun rose, they would offer us battle. This was agreed to by our side.

Meanwhile, the entire night was spent in dancing and singing, on both sides, with endless insults and other talk; such as, how little courage we had, how feeble a resistance we would make against their arms, and that, when day came, we should realize it to our ruin. Ours also were not slow in retorting, telling them they would see such execution of arms as never before, together with an abundance of such talk as is not unusual in the siege of a town.

After this singing, dancing, and bandying words on both sides to the fill, when day came, my companions and myself continued under cover, for fear that the enemy would see us. We arranged our arms in the best manner possible, being, however, separated, each in one of the canoes of the Montagnais. After arming ourselves with light armor, we each took an arquebuse, and went on shore.

I saw the enemy go out of their barricade, nearly two

hundred in number, stout and rugged in appearance. They
came at a slow pace towards us, with a dignity and assurance which greatly amused me, having three chiefs at their
head. Our men also advanced in the same order, telling me
that those who had three large plumes were the chiefs, and
that they had only these three, and that they could be distinguished by these plumes, which were much larger than
those of their companions, and that I should do what I
could to kill them. I promised to do all in my power, and
said that I was very sorry they could not understand me, so
that I might give order and shape to their mode of attacking
their enemies, and then we should, without doubt, defeat
them all; but that this could not now be obviated, and that I
should be very glad to show them my courage and goodwill
when we should engage in the fight.

As soon as we had landed, they began to run for some
two hundred paces towards their enemies, who stood firmly,
not having as yet noticed my companions, who went into
the woods with some savages. Our men began to call me
with loud cries; and, in order to give me a passageway, they
opened in two parts, and put me at their head, where I
marched some twentypaces in advance of the rest, until I
was within about thirty paces of the enemy, who at once
noticed me, and, halting, gazed at me, as I did also at them.
When I saw them making a move to fire at us, I rested my
musket against my cheek, and aimed directly at one of the
three chiefs. With the same shot, two fell to the ground; and
one of their men was so wounded that he died some time
after. I had loaded my musket with four balls. When our
side saw this shot so favorable for them, they began to raise
such loud cries that one could not have heard it thunder.
Meanwhile, the arrows flew on both sides.

The Iroquois were greatly astonished that two men had

been so quickly killed, although they were equipped with armor woven from cotton thread, and with wood which was proof against their arrows. This caused great alarm among them. As I was loading again, one of my companions fired a shot from the woods, which astonished them anew to such a degree that, seeing their chiefs dead, they lost courage, and took to flight, abandoning their camp and fort, and fleeing into the woods, whither I pursued them, killing still more of them. Our savages also killed several of them, and took ten or twelve prisoners. The remainder escaped with the wounded. Fifteen or sixteen were wounded on our side with arrow-shots; but they were soon healed.

AFTER GAINING THE VICTORY, our men amused themselves by taking a great quantity of Indian corn and some meal from their enemies, also their armor, which they had left behind that they might run better. After feasting sumptuously, dancing and singing, we returned three hours after, with the prisoners. The spot where this attack took place is in latitude 43° and some minutes, and the lake was called Lake Champlain.

After going some eight leagues, towards evening they took one of the prisoners, to whom they made a harangue, enumerating the cruelties which he and his men had already practised towards them without any mercy, and that, in like manner, he ought to make up his mind to receive as much. They commanded him to sing, if he had courage, which he did; but it was a very sad song.

Meanwhile, our men kindled a fire; and, when it was well burning, they each took a brand, and burned this poor creature gradually, so as to make him suffer greater torment. Sometimes they stopped, and threw water on his back.

Then they tore out his nails, and applied fire to the extremities of his fingers and private member. Afterwards, they flayed the top of hishead, and had a kind of gum poured all hot upon it; then they pierced his arms near the wrists, and, drawing up the sinews with sticks, they tore them out by force; but, seeing that they could not get them, they cut them. This poor wretch uttered terrible cries, and it excited my pity to see him treated in this manner, and yet showing such firmness that one would have said, at times, that he suffered hardly any pain at all.

They urged me strongly to take some fire, and do as they did. I remonstrated with them, saying that we practised no such cruelties, but killed them at once; and that, if they wished me to fire a musket-shot at him, I should be willing to do so. They refused, saying that he would not in that case suffer any pain. I went away from them, pained to see such cruelties as they practised upon his body. When they saw that I was displeased, they called me, and told me to fire a musket-shot at him. This I did without his feeling it, and thus put an end, by a single shot, to all the torments he would have suffered, rather than see him tyrannized over.

After his death, they were not yet satisfied, but opened him, and threw his entrails into the lake. Then they cut off his head, arms, and legs, which they scattered in different directions; keeping the scalp which they had flayed off, as they had done in the case of all the rest whom they had killed in the contest. They were guilty also of another monstrosity in taking his heart, cutting it into several pieces, and giving it to a brother of his to eat, as also to other prisoners: they took it into their mouths, but would not swallow it. Some Algonquin savages, who were guarding them, made some of them spit it out, when they threw it into the water. This is the manner in which these people behave towards those whom they capture in war, for whom it would be better to die fighting, or to kill themselves on the spur of the moment, as many do, rather than fall into the hands of their enemies.

After this execution, we set out on our return with the rest of the prisoners, who kept singing as they went along, with no better hopes for the future than he who had been so wretchedly treated.

Having arrived at the falls of the Iroquois, the Algonquins returned to their own country; so too the Ochateguins, with some of the prisoners: well satisfied with the results of the war, and that I had accompanied them so readily. We separated accordingly with loud protestations of mutual friendship; and they asked me whether I would not like to go into their country, to assist them with continued fraternal relations; and I promised that I would do so.

I returned with the Montagnais. After informing myself from the prisoners in regard to their country, and of its probable extent, we packed up the baggage for the return, which was accomplished with such despatch that we went every day in their canoes twenty-five or thirty leagues, which was their usual rate of travelling. When we arrived at the mouth of the river Iroquois, some of the savages dreamed that their enemies were pursuing them. This dream led them to move their camp forthwith, although the night was very inclement on account of the wind and rain; and they went and passed the remainder of the night, from fear of their enemies, amid high reeds on Lake St Peter. Two days after, we arrived at our settlement, where I gave them some bread and peas; also some beads, which they asked me for, in order to ornament the heads of their enemies, for the purpose of merrymaking upon their return.

The next day, I went with them in their canoes as far as

Tadoussac, in order to witness their ceremonies. On approaching the shore, they each took a stick, to the end of which they hung the heads of their enemies, who had been killed, together with some beads, all of them singing. When they were through with this, the women undressed themselves, so as to be in a state of entire nudity, when they jumped into the water, and swam to the canoes to take the heads of their enemies, which were on the ends of long poles before their boats: then they hung them about their necks, as if it had been some costly chain, singing and dancing meanwhile. Some days after, they presented me with one of these heads, as if it were something very precious; and also with a pair of arms taken from their enemies, to keep and show to the king. This, for the sake of gratifying them, I promised to do.

14

ROALD AMUNDSEN - EATING DOG ON
THE WAY TO THE SOUTH POLE, 1910-12

oald Engelbregt Gravning Amundsen (1872-1928)
was one of the world's greatest polar explorers. The
Norwegian beat Robert Scott, his British rival, to
become the first man to reach the South Pole, was the first to cross
the Northwest Passage, and led a pioneering expedition across the
Arctic Ocean.

Born to a family of Norwegian shipowners and sea captains,
he was put under pressure to become a doctor, a promise that
Amundsen kept only until his mother died when he was aged 21.
He then dedicated himself to his great passion: polar exploration,
inspired by early adventurers like Fridtjof Nansen and John
Franklin. As a young man, he slept with the windows open,
despite the freezing Norwegian winters, to condition himself for
the life he planned.

In 1909, Amundsen was organising a trip to try to be the first
man to reach the North Pole, when news reached him that the
Americans Robert Peary and Henson had beaten him to it. He
quickly, but secretly, changed his focus to the South Pole.

When Amundsen left Norway in June 1910 no one but his
brother and the ship's captain knew that he was heading for the

South Pole instead of the North. He sailed the Fram directly from the Madeira Islands to the Bay of Whales, Antarctica, along the Ross Sea. The base he set up there was 60 miles (100km) closer to the pole than Scott's base, and the route marginally less arduous. An experienced polar traveller, Amundsen had spent a long time with Inuit people, learning a lot about their way of life, Arctic survival techniques and sledging with Huskies, all of which would greatly help with his attempt on the South Pole. He prepared carefully for the coming journey, making a preliminary trip to deposit food supplies along the first part of his route to the pole and back. To transport his supplies, he used sled dogs, while Scott relied on Siberian ponies.

Amundsen set out with four companions, 52 dogs (some of whom would later be eaten by the explorers), and four sledges on October 19, 1911. After initially enjoying reasonably good weather, they were met by raging blizzards, thick fog and driving snow in 35mph winds. They pushed on, however, impelled by the fear that Scott might be ahead of them.

Overcoming their last major obstacle - traversing "The Devil's Ballroom", a glacier with a thin crust of snow covering a number of dangerous, deep crevasses - they finally arrived at the South Pole at 3pm on December 14, where the men, with weathered and frostbitten hands, grasped the Norwegian flag and planted it firmly in the ice. Amundsen named the plain King Haakon VII's Plateau. Leaving three days later, they safely reached their base at the Bay of Whales on January 25, 1912, having covered 1,860 miles in 99 days.

Scott, in the meantime, reached the South Pole on January 17, but on the return journey he and all his men perished.

Amundsen's triumph led him to be feted as one of the great polar explorers, and he revelled in being known as 'the last of the Vikings'. Controversy, particularly in Britain, over his secret change of plans in 1910 dogged him, however, as did questions *about his later feats. A senior official at the Royal Geographic Society described him as the most unhappy of all the polar explorers he had ever met. In June 1928, while searching for survivors of an airship disaster, Amundsen's plane crashed and he disappeared without a trace. He was 55. His body was never found.*

This edited extract published here, covering the final few days of the expedition, is taken from Amundsen's own account of it, published in 1912.

∼

'ALL THE QUALITIES I MOST ADMIRE IN MAN WERE NOW SHOWN: COURAGE AND DAUNTLESSNESS, WITHOUT BOASTING OR BIG WORDS'

AFTER WE HAD EXAMINED the conditions, and found out that on the following day if the weather permitted we should reach the plateau, we turned back, well satisfied with the result of our trip. We all agreed that we were tired, and longing to reach camp and get some food. The place where we turned was, according to the aneroid, 8,000 feet above the sea; we were therefore 2,500 feet higher than our tent down on the hill-side. Going down in our old tracks was easier work, though the return journey was somewhat monotonous. In many places the slope was rapid, and not a few fine runs were made. On approaching our camping ground, we had the sharpest descent, and here, reluctant as we might be, we found it wiser to put both our poles together and form a strong brake. We came down smartly enough, all the same.

It was a grand and imposing sight we had when we came

out on the ridge under which far below our tent stood. Surrounded on all sides by huge crevasses and gaping chasms, it could not be said that the site of our camp looked very inviting. The wildness of the landscape seen from this point is not to be described; chasm after chasm, crevasse after crevasse, with great blocks of ice scattered promiscuously about, gave one the impression that here Nature was too powerful for us. Here no progress was to be thought of. It was not without a certain satisfaction that we stood there and contemplated the scene. The little dark speck down there - our tent - in the midst of this chaos, gave us a feeling of strength and power. We knew in our hearts that the ground would have to be ugly indeed if we were not to manoeuvre our way across it and find a place for that little home of ours. Crash upon crash, roar upon roar, met our ears. Now it was a shot from Mount Nansen, now from one of the others; we could see the clouds of snow rise high into the air. The mountains were throwing off their winter mantles and putting on a more spring-like garb.

We came at a tearing pace down to the tent, where our companions had everything in most perfect order. The dogs lay snoring in the heat of the sun, and hardly condescended to move when we came scudding in among them. Inside the tent, a regular tropical heat prevailed; the sun was shining directly onto the red cloth and warming it. The Primus hummed and hissed, and the pemmican-pot bubbled and spurted. We desired nothing better in the world than to get in, fling ourselves down, eat, and drink. The news we brought was no trifling matter: the plateau tomorrow. It sounded almost too good to be true; we had reckoned that it would take us ten days to get up, and now we should do it in four. In this way we saved a great deal of dog food, as we should be able to slaughter the superfluous animals six days earlier than we had calculated. It was quite a little feast that evening in the tent; not that we had any more to eat than usual - we could not allow ourselves that - but the thought of the fresh dog cutlets that awaited us when we got to the top made our mouths water.

In course of time we had so habituated ourselves to the idea of the approaching slaughter that this event did not appear to us so horrible as it would otherwise have done. Judgment had already been pronounced, and the selection made of those who were worthy of prolonged life and those who were to be sacrificed. This had been, I may add, a difficult problem to solve, so efficient were they all.

THE RUMBLINGS CONTINUED ALL NIGHT, and one avalanche after another exposed parts of the mountain-sides that had been concealed from time immemorial. The following day, November 20, we were up and away at the usual time, about 8am. The weather was splendid, calm and clear. Getting up over the saddle was a rough beginning of the day for our dogs, and they gave a good account of themselves, pulling the sledges up with single teams this time. The going was heavy, as on the preceding day, and our advance through the loose snow was not rapid. We did not follow our tracks of the day before, but laid our course directly for the place where we had decided to attempt the ascent. As we approached Mount Ole Engelstad, under which we had to pass in order to come into the arm of the glacier between it and Mount Nansen, our excitement began to rise. What does the end look like? Does the glacier go smoothly on into the plateau, or is it broken up and impassable?

We rounded Mount Engelstad more and more; wider and wider grew the opening. The surface looked extremely good as it gradually came into view, and it did not seem as though our assumption of the previous day would be put to shame. At last the whole landscape opened out, and without obstruction of any kind whatever the last part of the ascent lay before us. It was both long and steep from the look of it, and we agreed to take a little rest before beginning the final attack.

We stopped right under Mount Engelstad in a warm and sunny place, and allowed ourselves on this occasion a little lunch, an indulgence that had not hitherto been permitted. The cooking case was taken out, and soon the Primus was humming in a way that told us it would not be long before the chocolate was ready. It was a heavenly treat, that drink. We had all walked ourselves warm, and our throats were as dry as tinder.

The contents of the pot were served round by the cook, [Helmer] Hanssen. It was no use asking him to share alike; he could not be persuaded to take more than half of what was due to him - the rest he had to divide among his comrades. The drink he had prepared this time was what he called chocolate, but I had some difficulty in believing him. He was economical, was Hanssen, and permitted no extravagance; that could be seen very well by his chocolate. Well, after all, to people who were accustomed to regard "bread and water" as a luxury, it tasted, as I have said, heavenly. It was the liquid part of the lunch that was served extra; if anyone wanted something to eat, he had to provide it himself - nothing was offered him. Happy was he who had saved some biscuits from his breakfast!

OUR HALT WAS NOT A VERY LONG one. It is a queer thing that, when one only has on light underclothing and windproof overalls, one cannot stand still for long without feeling cold. Although the temperature was no lower than 4°F, we were glad to be on the move again. The last ascent was fairly hard work, especially the first half of it. We never expected to do it with single teams, but tried it all the same.

For this last pull up I must give the highest praise both to the dogs and their drivers; it was a brilliant performance on both sides. I can still see the situation clearly before me. The dogs seemed positively to understand that this was the last big effort that was asked of them; they lay flat down and hauled, dug their claws in and dragged themselves forward. But they had to stop and get breath pretty often, and then the driver's strength was put to the test. It is no child's play to set a heavily-laden sledge in motion time after time. How they toiled, men and beasts, up that slope! But they got on, inch by inch, until the steepest part was behind them. Before them lay the rest of the ascent in a gentle rise, up which they could drive without a stop. It was stiff, nevertheless, and it took a long time before we were all up on the plateau on the southern side of Mount Engelstad.

We were very curious and anxious to see what the plateau looked like. We had expected a great, level plain, extending boundlessly towards the south; but in this we were disappointed. Towards the south-west it looked very level and fine, but that was not the way we had to go. Towards the south the ground continued to rise in long ridges running east and west, probably a continuation of the mountain chain running to the south-east, or a connection between it and the plateau. We stubbornly continued our march; we would not give in until we had the plain itself before us.

Our hope was that the ridge projecting from Mount Don Pedro Christophersen would be the last; we now had it before us. The going changed at once up here; the loose snow disappeared, and a few wind-waves (*sastrugi*) began to show themselves. These were specially unpleasant to deal with on this last ridge; they lay from south-east to north-west, and were as hard as flints and as sharp as knives. A fall among them might have had very serious consequences. One would have thought the dogs had had enough work that day to tire them, but this last ridge, with its unpleasant snow-waves, did not seem to trouble them in the least. We all drove up gaily, towed by the sledges, on to what looked to us like the final plateau, and halted at 8pm. The weather had held fine, and we could apparently see a very long way. In the far distance, extending to the north-west, rose peak after peak; this was the chain of mountains running to the south-east, which we now saw from the other side. In our own vicinity, on the other hand, we saw nothing but the backs of the mountains so frequently mentioned.

We afterwards learned how deceptive the light can be. I consulted the aneroid immediately on our arrival at the camping-ground, and it showed 10,920 feet above the sea, which the hypsometer afterwards confirmed. All the sledge-meters gave seventeen geographical miles, or thirty-one kilometres (nineteen and a quarter statute miles). This day's work - nineteen and a quarter miles, with an ascent of 5,750 feet - gives us some idea of what can be performed by dogs in good training. Our sledges still had what might be considered heavy loads; it seems superfluous to give the animals any other testimonial than the bare fact.

It was difficult to find a place for the tent, so hard was the snow up here. We found one, however, and set the tent. Sleeping-bags and kit-bags were handed in to me, as usual, through the tent-door, and I arranged everything inside. The cooking-case and the necessary provisions for that evening and the next morning were also passed in; but the part of my work that went more quickly than usual that night was getting the Primus started, and pumping it up to high-pressure. I was hoping thereby to produce enough noise to deaden the shots that I knew would soon be heard - twenty-four of our brave companions and faithful helpers were marked out for death. It was hard, but it had to be so. We had agreed to shrink from nothing in order to reach our goal. Each man was to kill his own dogs to the number that had been fixed.

THE PEMMICAN WAS COOKED REMARKABLY QUICKLY that evening, and I believe I was unusually industrious in stirring it. There went the first shot - I am not a nervous man, but I must admit that I gave a start. Shot now followed upon shot - they had an uncanny sound over the great plain. A trusty servant lost his life each time. It was long before the first man reported that he had finished; they were all to open their dogs, and take out the entrails to prevent the meat being contaminated. The entrails were for the most part devoured warm on the spot by the victims' comrades, so voracious were they all. Suggen, one of [Oscar] Wisting's dogs, was especially eager for warm entrails; after enjoying this luxury, he could be seen staggering about in a quite misshapen condition. Many of the dogs would not touch them at first, but their appetite came after a while.

The holiday humour that ought to have prevailed in the tent that evening - our first on the plateau - did not make its appearance; there was depression and sadness in the air - we had grown so fond of our dogs. The place was named the "Butcher's Shop". It had been arranged that we should stop here two days to rest and eat dog. There was more than one among us who at first would not hear of taking any part in this feast; but as time went by, and appetites became sharper, this view underwent a change, until, during the last few days before reaching the Butcher's Shop, we all thought and talked of nothing but dog cutlets, dog steaks, and the like. But on this first evening we put a restraint on ourselves; we thought we could not fall upon our four-footed friends and devour them before they had had time to grow cold.

We quickly found out that the Butcher's Shop was not a hospitable locality. During the night the temperature sank, and violent gusts of wind swept over the plain; they shook and tore at the tent, but it would take more than that to get a hold of it. The dogs spent the night in eating; we could hear the crunching and grinding of their teeth whenever we were awake for a moment. The effect of the great and sudden change of altitude made itself felt at once; when I wanted to turn round in my bag, I had to do it a bit at a time, so as not to get out of breath. That my comrades were affected in the same way, I knew without asking them; my ears told me enough.

It was calm when we turned out, but the weather did not look altogether promising; it was overcast and threatening. We occupied the forenoon in flaying a number of dogs. As I have said, all the survivors were not yet in a mood for dog's flesh, and it therefore had to be served in the most enticing form. When flayed and cut up, it went down readily all along the line; even the most fastidious then overcame their scruples. But with the skin on we should not have been able to persuade them all to eat that morning; probably this distaste was due to the smell clinging to the skins, and I must admit that it was not appetizing. The meat itself, as it lay there cut up, looked well enough, in all conscience; no butcher's shop could have exhibited a finer sight than we showed after flaying and cutting up ten dogs. Great masses of beautiful fresh, red meat, with quantities of the most tempting fat, lay spread over the snow. The dogs went round and sniffed at it. Some helped themselves to a piece; others were digesting. We men had picked out what we thought was the youngest and tenderest one for ourselves.

The whole arrangement was left to Wisting, both the selection and the preparation of the cutlets. His choice fell upon Rex, a beautiful little animal - one of his own dogs, by the way. With the skill of an expert, he hacked and cut away what he considered would be sufficient for a meal. I could not take my eyes off his work; the delicate little cutlets had an absolutely hypnotizing effect as they were spread out one by one over the snow. They recalled memories of old days, when no doubt a dog cutlet would have been less tempting than now - memories of dishes on which the cutlets were elegantly arranged side by side, with paper frills on the bones, and a neat pile of petis pois in the middle. Ah, my thoughts wandered still farther afield - but that does not concern us now, nor has it anything to do with the South Pole.

I was aroused from my musings by Wisting digging his axe into the snow as a sign that his work was done, after which he picked up the cutlets, and went into the tent. The clouds had dispersed somewhat, and from time to time the sun appeared, though not in its most genial aspect. We succeeded in catching it just in time to get our latitude determined 85° 36'S. We were lucky, as not long after the wind got up from the east-south-east, and, before we knew what was happening, everything was in a cloud of snow. But now we snapped our fingers at the weather; what difference did it make to us if the wind howled in the guy-ropes and the snow drifted? We had, in any case, made up our minds to stay here for a while, and we had food in abundance. We knew the dogs thought much the same: so long as we have enough to eat, let the weather go hang.

INSIDE THE TENT Wisting was getting on well when we came in after making these observations. The pot was on, and, to judge by the savoury smell, the preparations were already far advanced. The cutlets were not fried; we had neither frying-pan nor butter. We could, no doubt, have got some lard out of the pemmican, and we might have contrived some sort of a pan, so that we could have fried them if it had been necessary; but we found it far easier and quicker to boil them, and in this way we got excellent soup into the bargain. Wisting knew his business surprisingly well; he had put into the soup all those parts of the pemmican that contained most vegetables, and now he served us the finest fresh meat soup with vegetables in it. The *clou* of the repast was the dish of cutlets.

If we had entertained the slightest doubt of the quality of the meat, this vanished instantly on the first trial. The meat was excellent, quite excellent, and one cutlet after another disappeared with lightning-like rapidity. I must admit that they would have lost nothing by being a little more tender, but one must not expect too much of a dog. At this first meal I finished five cutlets myself, and I looked in vain in the pot for more. Wisting appeared not to have reckoned on such a brisk demand.

We employed the afternoon in going through our stock of provisions, and dividing the whole of it among three sledges; the fourth - [Sverre] Hassel's - was to be left behind. The provisions were thus divided.

Sledge No.1 (Wisting's) contained: Biscuits, 3,700 (daily

ration, 40 biscuits per man); Dogs' pemmican, 277 pounds (half a kilogram, or 1 pound 1 ounces per dog per day); Men's pemmican, 59 pounds (350 grams, or 12 ounces per man per day); Chocolate, 12 pounds (40 grams, or 1.4 ounces per man per day); Milk-powder, 13 pounds (60 grams, or 2.1 ounces per man per day).

The other two sledges had approximately the same supplies, and thus permitted us on leaving this place to extend our march over a period of sixty days with full rations. Our eighteen surviving dogs were divided into three teams, six in each. According to our calculation, we ought to be able to reach the Pole from here with these eighteen, and to leave it again with sixteen. Hassel, who was to leave his sledge at this point, thus concluded his provision account, and the divided provisions were entered in the books of the three others.

All this, then, was done that day on paper. It remained to make the actual transfer of provisions later, when the weather permitted. To go out and do it that afternoon was not advisable. Next day, November 23, the wind had gone round to the north-east, with comparatively manageable weather, so at seven in the morning we began to repack the sledges. This was not an altogether pleasant task; although the weather was what I have called "comparatively manageable", it was very far from being suitable for packing provisions.

The chocolate, which by this time consisted chiefly of very small pieces, had to be taken out, counted, and then divided among the three sledges. The same with the biscuits; every single biscuit had to be taken out and counted, and as we had some thousands of them to deal with, it will readily be understood what it was to stand there in about 4°F and a gale of wind, most of the time with bare hands, fumbling over this troublesome occupation. The wind increased while we were at work, and when at last we had finished, the snow was so thick that we could scarcely see the tent.

Our original intention of starting again as soon as the sledges were ready was abandoned. We did not lose very much by this; on the contrary, we gained on the whole. The dogs - the most important factor of all - had a thorough rest, and were well fed. They had undergone a remarkable change since our arrival at the Butcher's Shop; they now wandered about, fat, sleek and contented, and their former voracity had completely disappeared. As regards ourselves, a day or two longer made no difference; our most important article of diet, the pemmican, was practically left untouched, as for the time being dog had completely taken its place. There was thus no great sign of depression to be noticed when we came back into the tent after finishing our work, and had to while away the time.

As I went in, I could descry Wisting a little way off kneeling on the ground, and engaged in the manufacture of cutlets. The dogs stood in a ring round him, looking on with interest. The north-east wind whistled and howled, the air was thick with driving snow, and Wisting was not to be envied. But he managed his work well, and we got our dinner as usual. During the evening the wind moderated a little, and went more to the east; we went to sleep with the best hopes for the following day.

Saturday, November 25, came; it was a grand day in many respects. I had already seen proofs on several occasions of the kind of men my comrades were, but their conduct that day was such that I shall never forget it, to whatever age I may live. In the course of the night the wind had gone back to the north, and increased to a gale. It was blowing and snowing so that when we came out in the morning we could not see the sledges; they were half snowed under. The dogs had all crept together, and protected themselves as well as they could against the blizzard. The temperature was not so very low (-16.6°F), but low enough to be disagreeably felt in a storm.

We had all taken a turn outside to look at the weather, and were sitting on our sleeping-bags discussing the poor prospect. "It's the devil's own weather here at the Butcher's," said one, "it looks to me as if it would never get any better. This is the fifth day, and it's blowing worse than ever." We all agreed. "There's nothing so bad as lying weather-bound like this," continued another, "it takes more out of you than going from morning to night." I was of the same opinion. One day may be pleasant enough, but two, three, four, and, as it now seemed, five days? No, it was awful. "Shall we try it ?" No sooner was the proposal submitted than it was accepted unanimously and with acclamation. When I think of my four friends of the southern journey, it is the memory of that morning that comes first to my mind. All the qualities that I most admire in a man were clearly shown at that juncture: courage and dauntlessness, without boasting or big words. Amid joking and chaff, everything was packed, and then out into the blizzard.

IT WAS PRACTICALLY impossible to keep one's eyes open; the fine drift-snow penetrated everywhere, and at times one had a feeling of being blind. The tent was not only drifted up, but covered with ice, and in taking it down we had to handle it with care, so as not to break it in pieces. The dogs were not much inclined to start, and it took time to get them into their harness, but at last we were ready. One more glance over the camping-ground to see that nothing we ought to have with us had been forgotten. The fourteen dogs' carcasses that were left were piled up in a heap, and Hassel's sledge was set up against it as a mark. The spare sets of dog-harness, some Alpine ropes, and all our crampons for ice-work, which we now thought would not be required, were left behind. The last thing to be done was planting a broken ski upright by the side of the depot. It was Wisting who did this, thinking, presumably, that an extra mark would do no harm. That it was a happy thought the future will show.

And then we were off. It was a hard pull to begin with, both for men and beasts, as the high *sastrugi* continued towards the south, and made it extremely difficult to advance. Those who had sledges to drive had to be very attentive, and support them so that they did not capsize on the big waves, and we who had no sledges found great difficulty in keeping our feet, as we had nothing to lean against. We went on like this, slowly enough, but the main thing was that we made progress. The ground at first gave one the impression of rising, though not much. The going was extremely heavy; it was like dragging oneself through sand.

Meanwhile, the *sastrugi* grew smaller and smaller, and finally they disappeared altogether, and the surface became quite flat. The going also improved by degrees, for what reason it is difficult to say, as the storm continued unabated, and the drift now combined with falling snow was thicker than ever. It was all the driver could do to see his own dogs. The surface, which had become perfectly level, had the appearance at times of sinking; in any case, one would have thought so from the pace of the sledges. Now and again the dogs would set off suddenly at a gallop. The wind aft, no doubt, helped the pace somewhat, but it alone could not account for the change.

I did not like this tendency of the ground to fall away. In my opinion, we ought to have done with anything of that sort after reaching the height at which we were; a slight slope upward, possibly, but down no, that did not agree with my reckoning. So far the incline had not been so great as to cause uneasiness, but if it seriously began to go downhill, we should have to stop and camp. To run down at full gallop, blindly and in complete ignorance of the ground, would be madness. We might risk falling into some chasm before we had time to pull up.

Hanssen, as usual, was driving first. Strictly speaking, I should now have been going in advance, but the uneven surface at the start and the rapid pace afterwards had made it impossible to walk as fast the dogs could pull. I was therefore following by the side of Wisting's sledge, and chatting with him. Suddenly I saw Hanssen's dogs shoot ahead, and downhill they went at the wildest pace, Wisting after them. I shouted to Hanssen to stop, and he succeeded in doing so by twisting his sledge. The others, who were following, stopped when they came up to him. We were in the middle of a fairly steep descent; what there might be below was not easy to decide, nor would we try to find out in that weather.

Was it possible that we were on our way down through the mountains again? It seemed more probable that we lay on one of the numerous ridges; but we could be sure of nothing before the weather cleared. We trampled down a place for the tent in the loose snow, and soon got it up. It was not a long day's march that we had done - eleven and three-quarter miles - but we had put an end to our stay at the Butcher's Shop, and that was a great thing. The boiling-point test that evening showed that we were 10,300 feet above the sea, and that we had thus gone down 620 feet from the Butcher's.

We turned in and went to sleep. As soon as it brightened, we should have to be ready to jump out and look at the weather; one has to seize every opportunity in these regions. If one neglects to do so, it may mean a long wait and much may be lost. We therefore all slept with one eye open, and we knew well that nothing could happen without our noticing it.

At three in the morning, the sun cut through the clouds and we through the tent-door. To take in the situation was more than the work of a moment. The sun showed as yet like a pat of butter, and had not succeeded in dispersing the thick mists; the wind had dropped somewhat, but was still fairly strong. This is, after all, the worst part of one's job - turning out of one's good, warm sleeping-bag, and standing outside for some time in thin clothes, watching the weather.

We knew by experience that a gleam like this, a clearing in the weather, might come suddenly, and then one had to be on the spot. The gleam came; it did not last long, but long enough: we lay on the side of a ridge that fell away pretty steeply. The descent on the south was too abrupt, but on the south-east it was better and more gradual, and ended in a wide, level tract.

We could see no crevasses or unpleasantness of any kind. It was not very far that we could see, though; only our nearest surroundings. Well content with our morning's work, we turned in again and slept till 6am, when we began our morning preparations. The weather, which had somewhat improved during the night, had now broken loose again, and the north-easter was doing all it could. However, it would take more than storm and snow to stop us now.

Printed in Great Britain
by Amazon